The Inferior Sex

THE
INFERIOR SEX

WALLACE REYBURN

PRENTICE-HALL, INC.
Englewood Cliffs, New Jersey

Printed in the United States of America
Prentice-Hall International, Inc., London
Prentice-Hall of Australia, Pty. Ltd., North Sydney
Prentice-Hall of Canada, Ltd., Toronto
Prentice-Hall of India Private Ltd., New Delhi
Prentice-Hall of Japan, Inc., Tokyo

Library of Congress Cataloging in Publication Data

Reyburn, Wallace.
    The inferior sex.

    1. Woman—History and condition of women. I. Title.
HQ1154.R48   301.41′2   72-5750
ISBN 0-13-464321-6

ACKNOWLEDGMENTS

Acknowledgment is made to the following for their kind permission to reprint material from copyright sources: The Olympia Press Inc., New York, and The Olympia Press Ltd., London [*S.C.U.M. (Society for Cutting Up Men) Manifesto* by Valerie Solanas, with an introduction by Vivian Gornick]; William Morrow & Co. Inc., New York, and Weidenfeld & Nicolson Ltd., London (*Jerusalem the Golden* by Margaret Drabble); William Morrow & Co. Inc., New York, and Jonathan Cape Ltd., London (*The Dialectic of Sex* by Shulamith Firestone); Doubleday & Company Inc., New York, and George Allen & Unwin Ltd., London (*Utopian Motherhood* by Robert T. Francoeur).

Extract from the *Daily Express* article "How to Face Up to Your Complexion" by Mary Collins reproduced by kind permission of Beaverbrook Newspapers.

From *The Female Eunuch* by Germaine Greer. Copyright © 1970 by Germaine Greer. Used with permission of McGraw-Hill Book Company and MacGibbon & Kee Ltd.

Acknowledgment is made to Penguin Books Ltd. for permission to reprint an excerpt from Alice Heim: *Intelligence and Personality*. Copyright © Alice W. Heim, 1970.

CONTENTS

PART TWO

The Feminine Syndrome

The Inferior Sex

PART ONE

FACTS
THE
FEMINISTS
PREFER
TO
IGNORE

I   IN THE SHADOW OF MEN

When I read that a theatrical company which for many years has been dedicated to producing the work of the great playwrights had decided to put on its first play by a woman I could not help but feel that it had taken them a long time to get around to it.

It stood to reason, of course, because there are no great women playwrights, no feminine equivalent of Shakespeare, Sheridan, or Shaw, Molière, Ibsen, or Eugene O'Neill. Men write the great plays.

The reason why women are not mentally equipped to write worthwhile plays is gone into later. The point I would make here is that if the male domination of playwriting were an isolated fact, women could say with justification: "So what?" But it is not isolated. The shattering truth is that men outshine women in *every* field of endeavor.

If one would put this statement to the test all one need do is think of any pursuit—designing buildings, say, or composing music or inventing things—and then think of how many famous names in that field one can bring to mind. At once you will think of dozens of men, and be hard put to think of any women.

Having tried to think of a great woman architect, composer, or inventor, try philosophy. With a flood of names like Socrates, Plato, Schopenhauer, Nietzsche, and John Stuart Mill pouring into one's mind, who are the women philosophers? There has never been one.

Medicine, law, religion, science . . . right on through all the spheres of human endeavor one racks one's brains to think of women who have been in the forefront. And the pitiful contribution by women to the advancement, well-being, comfort, and pleasure of mankind is even more astounding when one realizes that they are not even any good in what should be regarded as the feminine corridors of power.

Obstetrics, for instance. You couldn't name anything more definitely a woman's domain, literally and figuratively. Yet it is men who have evolved all the advanced techniques, treatments, and operations. Women have not contributed a jot to this essentially female sphere of medicine.

All the way along the line of the so-called feminine pursuits it is men who dominate—child care (Spock, etc.), cooking (ever hear of a woman chef in a top restaurant?), designing clothes (Dior, etc.), poetry (Milton, etc.), typing (world champion: Albert Tangora), etc.

One cannot help but paraphrase the popular song by saying that anything women can do, men can do better.

In the following chapter I give a cross section of the failure of women to live up to men in every field. But it would be unfair, not to say monotonous, merely to list the feminine inadequacies. I have endeavored to analyze *why* they have fallen so short of men in each sphere and where possible, even though it might be regarded as presumptuous on my part, I have suggested ways in which women can make a better showing.

Likewise, in the second section of the book I have tried to be constructive. This part examines the feminine syndrome, *i.e.*, the biological and psychological influences which bear on the female and make her interestingly—albeit tantalizingly and at times infuriatingly—different from the superior sex. Women may find some helpful advice there. More helpful, I dare to suggest, than a great proportion of what their own liberationists are putting forward on their behalf.

For the record, although I am sure that there cannot be many people who have failed to notice, women were emancipated just following World War I, and after a lapse of half a century in which their emancipation was not seen to be doing them much good, militant feminists banded together under the banner of the Women's Liberation movement to make a fresh effort, whether the bulk of women liked it or not, to jolt them into assertive action against "male domination."

Not for one moment would one claim that the movement is not achieving anything. The Women's Libbers are doing some very good work. I hear, for example, that a large downtown eating place in one of our larger cities barred unescorted females from midnight onward. The reason for this was that they felt justifiably hurt when they were accused and convicted of harboring prostitutes. Women's Lib went to work on this discrimination against women. The restaurant was forced to lift the ban. Women's Lib got the whores back in.

We will naturally have more to say in due course about Women's Liberation, particularly the underlying false premise of the movement—that people can be changed in their innate approach to life by legislation, that by getting laws passed and hindrances removed, women will achieve things which they are not equipped to do or have no interest in doing.

The main object of this book is not to denigrate women. It is to confront the feminists with unassailable facts which will stop them, for heaven's sake, from going on and on about equality and make them come to realize that the true function of women is to find enduring happiness in being secondary to men.

As Freud so aptly put it: "For both partners to be equal is a practical impossibility. There must be inequality and the superiority of the man is the lesser of the two evils."

2 THE ABC OF WOMEN'S INFERIORITY

ARCHITECTS

Men	*Women*
Ictinus and Callicrates (Parthenon)	Elizabeth Whitfield Scott
Anthemius and Isodorus (St. Sophia)	
Brunelleschi (Duomo)	
Buonorotti (Dome of St. Peter's)	
Le Vau and Jules Mansard (Versailles)	
Palladio	
Inigo Jones	
Christopher Wren	
Robert Adam	
John Nash	
Sir Edwin L. Lutyens	
Le Corbusier	
Frank Lloyd Wright	
Sir Basil Spence	
etc., etc.	

In 1927 there was an open competition for British and American architects to submit designs for a new playhouse to replace the burned-out Shakespearean theater at Stratford-on-Avon. Seventy-three architects entered and one design was unanimously selected by the assessors; Bernard Shaw, seconding the adoption of their report, said that "it was the only possible design, a very good one, and the only one that showed any theatre sense."

The competition had been conducted in the customary British manner—the names of all those submitting designs were withheld from the judges until after they had made their decision. So it came as something of a surprise when it was revealed that the winner was a woman—the solitary female among the seventy-three competing architects. Elizabeth Whitfield Scott, of Bournemouth, member of a family of distinguished architects, had indeed struck a dramatic blow for the feminists.

But it is terribly isolated. There have been and are other women architects but it is a long journey between standing examples of their work. And no woman of course has ever designed (or is likely to) anything as impressive as the Taj Mahal or Notre Dame cathedral. Anything such as the dome of St. Paul's would be quite beyond them, for architecture is not just a matter of drawing pretty pictures. It involves higher mathematics and engineering, which are not feminine spheres. (At school, Elizabeth Whitfield Scott was good at sums, which helped.)

However, even if the big concept is outside the scope of women, one would have thought that the designing of houses would be something right in their laps. After all, it is they who spend more time than anybody else in houses.

But although women are unhappy about so many things about house design, they don't say to men: "Move over and let *us* plan the sort of homes *we* want." They just complainingly put up with houses designed by men without women in mind.

If women did their own designing—and got everything they want and need—there would be many radical changes. For example, they would think about *baby carriages* when planning their houses or apartments. Men never do. Not being encumbered with that problem in their personal lives, male architects just ignore the whole thing. Even though they have to stumble over the damn carriages in hallways not designed to accommodate them, men still don't allocate in the blueprints an area set apart for parking them.

And more than that. Getting the confounded conveyance in and out of the house. It is a convention of architecture that you go up steps to get into a house. Rattle, bang, crash, getting the baby carriage up and down those steps, while poor junior in there wonders what sort of bumpy world he has been born into. The men who build safety islands in the middle of streets have at least, but only in recent years, realized that a woman crossing the street with a baby carriage should have a section of the island which remains at street level so that she doesn't have to do an up-and-over act to negotiate the island. But this message hasn't reached male architects. If women designed the houses they would have at least one entrance to the house that was at ground level, or failing that, a ramp beside the steps for this special use.

And the matter of somewhere to hang out laundry. For generations women have put up with the fact that men, when designing a home, never make adequate provision for the important consideration of a place to hang things out to dry—ideally a spot that catches the sun *and* wind and is screened off from view. Almost invariably the rigging up of such facilities has of necessity been an improvisation by the householder after the house has been completed. The dryer came to the rescue of the architects, in that they could argue that the old-fashioned clothesline is now completely outdated. But it isn't true. Women are forever taking it into their heads to wash out a slip or a brassiere or other odd item without going through the whole washing machine and dryer rigmarole. And so . . . they sit in the garden there entertaining a friend with coffee against the background of their laundered undies waving in the breeze on a line stretched from a drainpipe to a nearby tree.

And facilities inside the home. What lasting improvements women could make if they had the initiative to take over from male designers.

Electric wall sockets—why are they always located down by the floor, so that women, who are the greatest users of them, always have to stoop when they use them? This applies especially to plugs for ironing and vacuuming. Why not position the sockets up on the wall? Unsightly, you say? But what about when a man plugs in his electric razor? There, handily placed up on the wall, is the socket for *his* electric appliance. He has seen to that, and has not given a thought to women having to bend down over and over again when operating their vacuum or iron.

And the plug itself, which you fit into the socket—what an irritating, often infuriating business it is getting the prongs securely inserted correctly into position, particularly when you are reaching down behind a couch or under a bed or some other similar location that you can't even see. Today the camera and the tape recorder have been tremendously simplified by the introduction of cassettes which eliminate all the finicky messing around with spools of film and tape. Why not adapt the cassette principle to electric plugs, so that automatically the plug goes in correctly and can go in no other way?

Consider a simple thing like the drain in the bath. Men certainly didn't have the overworked housewife in mind when they positioned it directly under the faucets. She is cleaning the bath. As the water gushes forth she has to sluice it up with her hand into the tub to prevent it from going down the drain. Then the dirty water from her cleaning has to compete with fresh water from the faucets to empty into it. How much simpler and more practical for the drain to be at the other end of the bath. What a saving in time and effort with the incoming water cooperating with the housewife on its way along the bath to the outlet.

And kitchen cupboards—why stoop down to fumble around among the shelves for what you want, or for that

matter why have to reach up on tiptoe to get at things in
what are supposed to be the modern, accessible kitchen cupboards at eye level? If women were smart they would be
inspired by what man has done for himself with tool closets
which open up into easily get-atable layers and *hors d'oeuvres*
carts to be seen in restaurants, where the waiter doesn't have
to bend down to display and serve the various items, they
swing up to waist height with a flick of the wrist. Why not
adapt that principle to the kitchen cabinet and put an end to
the hide-and-seek game women have to play when they're
looking for the curry powder or the soy sauce they know
they've got *somewhere*?

And bedmaking. Just think of all the man-hours, or rather
woman-hours, taken up by this tedious chore, probably the
most boring of all the household jobs. But why should it
have to be such a laborious operation? Why, today, can it not
be radically simplified as have so many other things? Why do
we adhere to the age-old convention that our sleeping equipment should consist of four to eight assorted sheets, blankets
and other covers? When we go camping we use just the one
simple unit—the sleeping bag. Why not adapt this to household use? With all the new synthetic fabrics in existence it
should be the simplest thing in the world to evolve an attractive single-unit sleeping container, in summer and winter
weights, which could be readily aired and laundered. Men, the
great inventors (see under *Inventions*), are not confronted
with the daily boredom of bedmaking so they have not bothered to turn their minds to simplifying the whole thing; and
women, not being inventive, just put up with it.

But that, sad to say, is a female characteristic. They will
complain endlessly about such things as nowhere to hang out
laundry, badly placed electric sockets, and so on, but will do
nothing about taking the whole thing over themselves and
righting the wrongs.

ARTISTS

Men	*Women*
Leonardo da Vinci	Grandma Moses
Michelangelo	
Botticelli	
Titian	
Canaletto	
Rubens	
Rembrandt	
El Greco	
Velasquez	
Reynolds	
Gainsborough	
Constable	
Turner	
Matisse	
Degas	
Renoir	
Gauguin	
Van Gogh	
Whistler	
Grant Wood	
Dali	
Picasso	
etc., etc.	

Why women can't paint, only the good Lord knows. It isn't as if, over the centuries, they have been prevented from doing so because being an artist required having degrees or other special qualifications denied to women. Anyone who can get hold of charcoal, crayon, or paint can be an artist. And no great intellect is required. As witness the splendid wall paintings of the Australian Aborigines, who are among the most backward and under-privileged of the world's races.

Circulating in any of the great art galleries, seeking hopefully for something by a woman among the row upon row of paintings by men, one can only conclude that women have an inborn inability to commit to canvas anything that commands our attention.

COMEDIANS

Men   *Women*

Ed Wynn   Phyllis Diller
Clark and McCullough   Joan Rivers
Wheeler and Wolsey
Jack Benny
Fred Allen
Bob Hope
Godfrey Cambridge
Shelley Berman
Bob Newhart
Mort Sahl
Lenny Bruce
Danny Thomas
Milton Berle
Dick Gregory
etc., etc.

You may ask where, in the list above, is the greatest internationally known comedian of all time—Charlie Chaplin? He is not left out just to let women off lightly, since they have never produced anything approaching him. The list is devoted merely to one aspect of comedy, what for want of a better name is called the stand-up comic, *i.e.*, the comedian whose stock in trade is the telling of jokes. I have taken this sphere of comedy because, as we shall see, it has a broader application, it touches on a characteristic of women which we encounter every day.

One would not suggest for one moment that women are

unable to make an audience laugh. Bea Lillie has had at least two generations in stitches with comic songs such as *Wind Around My Heart*. Through the years there have been such wonderful dizzy dames and dumb blondes as Zazu Pitts, Billie Burke, Judy Holliday, and Goldie Hawn. Few can wring more out of a comic situation more adroitly than Lucille Ball. Women can deliver superbly the comedy scripts men write for them.

But there is a big gap, that field of comedy well nigh unpopulated by women. Where are the female equivalents of Bob Hope and Jack Benny? Where are the women who can stand alone on a stage and reel off jokes and have an audience rolling in the aisles, for an hour or more if need be?

The art of the stand-up comic has long been quite foreign to women. Phyllis Diller and Joan Rivers seem in modern times to be the only ones capable of showing others of their sex that it *can* be done.

Why can't women tell jokes, either to amuse an audience or in everyday life?

The fundamental reason lies in the fact that they suffer from the "How Am I Doing?" complex which we deal with fully later. Visually it is inherent in them not to do anything that will make them look foolish, lose their dignity. There has never been any feminine equivalent of the "red-nosed comedians" of vaudeville days, the outlandish getup of Clark and McCullough, no female counterpart of the "baggy pants" clowns. That would cut across the in-built desire of women to look their best at all times. Verbally there is the constant dread of "what will people think." To embark on a story and make a hash of it would make them the focal point of ridicule, so that when they do pluck up the courage to relate an anecdote they are so self-conscious during the course of it that a man will suffer the stumblings solely in the hope that there will be a good payoff and he'll be able to fix it up and tell it properly later.

Being objective in their approach to life, men never suffer from this "How Am I Doing?" complex. They'll go in feet first and if things do go adrift they'll join in the laughter at their expense. As an example I remember Bennett Cerf telling me of the local dignitary who used to have his speeches written for him. On one occasion he was so busy that he had to get on to the platform without having the chance to read through what had been prepared for him. In the course of the speech he came to a section that read: "Which reminds me of one of my favorite stories, which concerns—" It so happened that it was a story he had never heard before, and he laughed so much at it that he broke his glasses and somebody else had to read the rest of his speech for him.

Women's ineptitude as raconteurs is compounded by the fact that they can't remember jokes properly. Having been told that well-known limerick that starts "There was a young man named Skinner, who invited his girl friend to dinner . . ." they decide to be the hit of the evening by recounting it, and having sailed off happily with "There was a young man named Tupper, who invited his girl friend to supper . . ." they then wonder why it doesn't seem to work out the way they'd heard it.

Only in the field of unconscious humor do they shine. Their naiveté is such that time and again they can be screamingly funny without realizing that they are. The perfect example of this is the *Children's Hour* radio script prepared by an old dear who gave it the title of "Playing With Your Balls." It concerned a game she evolved for children, with musical accompaniment, in which they were asked to prance around the room, those with little balls flicking them up in the air (tingalingaling) and those with big balls throwing them up and letting them drop (boomboomboom). The female producer of the program saw nothing amiss with it and as it went out on the air the male engineers at the radio station kept their fingers crossed that it wouldn't suddenly dawn on her so that she would abruptly cut it off, for they knew that a pirated recording of "Playing With Your Balls" would become a collectors' item. As indeed it has, and anyone lucky enough to have a record of it finds it a never failing hit as a party piece.

COMPOSERS

Men	*Women*
Purcell	Carrie Jacobs-Bond
Scarlatti	(she wrote *I Love You*
Bach	*Truly*)
Mozart	
Beethoven	
Schubert	
Brahms	
Berlioz	
Wagner	
Verdi	
Gounod	
Rossini	
Tschaikovsky	
Debussy	
Elgar	
Sibelius	
etc., etc.	

It is a shocking state of affairs when you think that for four hundred years composers have been turning out great musical works—symphonies, concertos, chamber music, oratorios, operas—and all the composers are men. It is staggering when one looks at the vast library of the world's great music as displayed so colorfully in the array of albums at a record shop, to survey all that and realize that not a single note of it has been written by a woman. Confronted by that damning evidence one wonders how feminists have the effrontery to talk of equality of the sexes.

It cannot be argued that the composing of music has been a closed shop. Anyone, male or female, can have musical ideas and develop them. Just as no man was able to say to the Brontë sisters, "You are forbidden from thinking up plots for novels and developing them," so it would have been impossible for men to prevent the emergence of a female equivalent of Strauss, who was composing his waltzes at the same time the Brontës were writing their books.

It is not men who have stopped women from being great composers. It lies with women themselves. They have never got anywhere in musical composition and never will because of this simple fact: Music is mathematics and woman hasn't a mathematical bone in her body.

It is one thing to get a musical idea; it is quite another thing to write it down. You have to know that the notes of the scale are separated by a full tone, except the third and fourth, and the seventh and eighth, which in each case are separated by a semitone. To find the key which has one sharp you go up five notes to G, which has to have its seventh note (F) sharpened, so that there is a semitone between it and the G, and to find the key with two sharps you go up five notes from G to D, and so on up by fifths to get all your keys with sharps, going down by fifths from C in similar fashion to find your keys with flats. And that's just finding your way around the various scales! After that the complications really start and you are in a world of dominant sevenths, triads, chromatic progressions, counterpoint, atonality, the five-note scale, exposition and recapitulation—such a labyrinth of technicalities that they are quite beyond the grasp of women.

There is no female counterpart of Beethoven's Fifth Symphony for the simple reason that you cannot expect a person who is incapable of fixing an ordinary electric fuse to be able to issue an hour and a half of written instructions to an eighty-piece orchestra.

SONGWRITERS

Men	Women
Irving Berlin	?
Cole Porter	
George and Ira Gershwin	

Jimmy McHugh
De Sylva, Brown and Henderson
Hoagy Carmichael
Ray Noble
Rodgers and Hart
Rodgers and Hammerstein
Jerome Kern
Frank Loesser
Noel Coward
Lerner and Loewe
Lennon and McCartney
Burt Bacharach
Henry Mancini
Lionel Bart
etc., etc.

If one accepts that the intricacies of composing serious music are beyond the grasp of the female mind, what then of the popular song? Why so lamentable the creative contribution of women to what used to be called the "Hit Parade" and is now the "Charts"?

Nothing could be more simple of structure and demanding of so little time in gestation as the pop number. Rodgers, of the Rodgers and Hammerstein duo, has said that if he can't get a song worked out in twenty minutes he abandons it and goes on to another idea. But Rodgers, it might be argued, is a trained musician. In this regard, that's not an essential. Time and again smash hits have come from the "one finger artist." You don't even need to peck it out on the piano. Consider the example of Lionel Bart, British songsmith and writer of musicals, whose *Oliver!* on stage and screen, if not quite another *My Fair Lady* or *Sound of Music* is at least up in that category as a hit show. Bart unashamedly admits to *humming* his tunes for somebody else to write down.

From the aspiring Gershwin and youthful Irving Berlin on through to the Beatles, numerous are the song-hit writers who have needed someone to "sole and heel" their numbers

for them, as they say in the trade. There's nothing at all
wrong with that. After all, it's the musical idea that's important in a pop song—the catchy tune. Knocking it into shape
technically is something that any musician can do.

So, without technical knowledge or musical training required, why is it that women haven't been thinking up good
tunes? It is certainly not because the popular song is something that they are not interested in, as with weight lifting,
say, or designing racing cars.

Early in life it was brought home to me just how meaning-
ful the popular song is to women. I was staying with my
mother and sister in London when a very plausible young
Indian from Madras came on the scene. He was kicking up his
heels at the time, having just been sent down from Cambridge. My sister fell heavily for him, which didn't go down
well with my mother. I don't think it was so much that he
was an Indian; in New Zealand we live happily enough among
our Maoris. Nor do I think she minded too much about Cambridge feeling that he had not been working hard enough at
his studies. I think what really put him beyond the pale as far
as she was concerned was one evening when he said to her:
"Would you like a chocolate?" And he took his handkerchief
from his pocket, unfolded it, and proffered a cluster of can-
dies. So as not to hurt his feelings, she took one, still warm
from his body heat, and saying she would save it for after
dinner she made some excuse to withdraw and it finished up
among the hydrangeas.

My mother felt that it was fortunate that shortly after this
we sailed for New Zealand; my sister would be separated
from her Indian prince and, it was to be hoped, would eventually forget about him. For her part, my sister shut herself
in her cabin for what seemed like the whole trip and played
the Ethel Waters record of "Love Me or Leave Me" over and
over and over.

Anything that can provide solace in that way must be
important to women. For generations the popular song has
been doing sterling work for females in the mending of a

broken heart; affording musical accompaniment for the new affair (Our song!); furnishing entertainment for the bobbed-haired flappers on the old crank-handle portable on the beach (Damn! We forgot to bring needles!); for jitterbugging to Kay Kayser; and lying in the bath with the Beatles belting it out on the transistor radio perched on the side of the tub.

The popular song is an important component of the female way of life. But what have they ever done about contributing to the production of the swing-bop-rock numbers they've always loved to listen to? Women love historical novels, so for years there have been batches of females churning out reams of this commodity for the enjoyment of those of their sex. Why on earth haven't they been doing the same thing in the field of the popular song?

It isn't as if the popular music industry were closed to them. As performers they are in and out of the recording studios, on the air, in nightclubs, singing away on an equal footing with men. In fact they have an advantage over men. They are permitted to sing men's songs and get away with it. Gracie Fields, for instance. Her biggest hit was the one in which she sang about her undying love for "Sally," without anyone ever imputing any lesbian tendencies to her. Yet what man would come on and dare to sing "He's Just My Bill"? Through the years women have shown themselves capable at any given time of monopolizing the Top Ten, in the person of such as Ethel Merman, Rosemary Clooney, Judy Garland, Lena Horne, Eartha Kitt, and Shirley Bassey.

And equal pay? But of course. Try to tell Shirley Bassey that she must accept a lower fee for her Las Vegas appearance because she's a woman.

So women are right in there in the pop music business, *but only as performers*. That's the crux of the whole matter. As long as the men write the songs for them, they'll sing 'em.

There *was* one woman who wrote a successful popular song. I can't for the life of me remember her name but I do know that she was a Toronto girl. Toronto is noted for at least two things. One is the prudishness of its women, which has given rise to the oft-quoted comment, "The girls of Toronto are hard to get onto." Its other claim to fame is its annual Exhibition, the largest permanent city fair in the world. A feature of the Toronto "Ex" in the old days was the importing of the big U.S. name bands—the Dorseys, Artie Shaw, Guy Lombardo, Whiteman, and so on—to play for the delight of the bobby-soxers and other young people assembled in huge tents.

During the Ex of 1936 our girl got a musician to write down a song she had written and she took it in her hot little hand to Tommy Dorsey. He liked it. He played it. He recorded it. *I'll Never Smile Again* went to the top of the Hit Parade of 1936.

Some twenty years later the heroine of our little saga was inspired to write a follow-up, which I think was called *I'll Never Cry Again*. It didn't do much. She'd shot her bolt in 1936.

But the point is that she was just an ordinary female (a nurse, if I recall rightly) of no musical experience who made the grade with a hit song.

She demonstrated for others of her sex to see, that it *can* be done. There is nothing at all to stop women from being successful songwriters. The fact that they are not, that musically they are content merely to be parasites living off the creative talents of men, highlights a basic flaw in the approach of the Women's Liberation movement.

This is something which I shall iterate and reiterate throughout this book, since it is a fundamental of the faulty attitude of the feminine militants.

The whole basis of their attempt to change the lot of women is to do it by legislation, in its broadest sense, *i.e.*, to remove the man-made barriers against women in all sorts of spheres of influence. They appear to think that overnight, the moment women are legislated to full equality of opportunity, they will as if by magic demonstrate achievement as great as that of men. Men are the evil people who must be stopped from hampering female talent, initiative, and drive.

But why don't the feminists take time out to look around at their own kind and take note that for generation after generation they have just sat around and done nothing in fields that are wide open to them—songwriting being just one of the many? Instead of having the evil male in their sights all the time, does it never occur to them to turn on their own sex and say: "For God's sake, it's making it tough for us to get you liberated when you're slothful in the fields already open to you."

HOUSEHOLD WORDS
(derived from the names of the originators)

Men	*Women*
sandwich	bloomers
braille	
morse	
galvanize	
pasteurize	
platonic	
stetson	
cardigan	
macintosh	
macadam	
boycott	
saxophone	
diesel	
etc., etc.	

There cannot be many people who do not know how the sandwich came into being and why it is called a *sandwich* rather than, say, a *quickmeal* or other such coinage. But for the sake of those who don't know, the explanation is that the third Earl of Sandwich was an inveterate gambler, so addicted to the gaming tables that he resented the time wasted in leaving them to go off and sit down to a meal. So, in a sudden flash of inspiration, he instructed the kitchen staff to cut two slices of bread, place some meat in between, and serve it to him while he gambled uninterrupted.

The *dagwood*, the ten-tier glorification of the sandwich, of course came later but the principle was the same: a man gets a bright idea and his name, associated with his product becomes a household word incorporated into the language without a capital letter.

"James Bond was *galvanized* into action" sounds modern enough, but actually *galvanize* had its origin two centuries ago when Luigi Galvani (1737-1798) conducted a series of experiments at Bologna University. These presaged the plating of metal by the action of an electrical current, as with *galvanized* iron in its original form, and hence—James Bond leaping into activity as if stimulated by an electric shock.

And just as Galvani is still getting a credit line two hundred years later we are also paying credit to Louis Pasteur (1822-1895) whenever we pick up a bottle of *pasteurized* milk and to James Watt (1736-1819) every time we talk about the *wattage* of an electric lamp.

One could go on endlessly enumerating the wonderful service done to mankind by the introduction of raised printing for the blind (Louis *Braille*, 1809-1852), the laboratory burner (Robert *Bunsen*, 1811-1899), the S.O.S. signal (Samuel *Morse*, 1791-1872), the safety loading line for ships (Samuel *Plimsoll*, 1824-1898), and all the other names of men now in everyday use.

But when one comes to line up on the other side all the women who have left their names implanted in our language the staggering fact emerges that there is only one: Mrs. Amelia Bloomer (1818-1894). Search as diligently as you may, you will find the name of no other woman which has become an everyday word. It is a sad commentary on the paucity of women's contribution to the welfare of mankind that the one solitary word in our language derived from a woman's name is *bloomers*.

INVENTORS
(and Discoverers)

Men

Women

Alexander Graham Bell
  telephone, 1876

Marie (and Pierre) Curie
  radium, 1898

Elijah Galloway
  linoleum, 1843

Wilhelm Röntgen
  X rays, 1895

Sir Joseph Swan
  artificial silk, 1883

Sir Alexander Fleming
  penicillin, 1928

Nehemiah Grew
  Epsom salts, 1695

Thomas Edison
  phonograph, 1877

Sir Frank Whittle
  jet propulsion, 1930-41

Thomas Saint
  sewing machine, 1790

Sir Isaac Newton
  law of gravity, 1685

Dr. Eugene Wildiers
  vitamins, 1901

etc., etc.

Women are almost totally uninventive. If you look around you at the electric light, the telephone, the refrigerator, the television set and all the other things that make life easier, safer, or more interesting you may be 99.9 percent sure that nothing your eye lights upon was invented by a woman.

Junior Pears Encyclopedia (the British reference book for children, which is of inestimable help to grown-ups) lists 235

inventions which have contributed to the welfare, health, and
general comfort of mankind and only two and one-half of
those they list from Acetylene to X rays were invented by
women.

That pitiful showing is bad enough, but it is even worse
when one notes which the two and a half inventions were.
Granted Madame Marie Curie's half credit for discovering radium with her husband, Pierre, is an outstanding thing, something to which women can point with justifiable pride and
which they do, over and over again (see Chapter 4). But what
are the other two which vie with Fleming's discovery of penicillin, Jansen's microscope, and Whittle's jet engine? Well, it
seems that women's two other great inventors were a Miss
Glover, who invented the tonal sol-fa in 1841, and Bertha
Upton, who in 1896 invented the golliwog, the black rag doll
popular until deemed racist.

Women cannot even cope with the inventions which men
have lavished upon them. Men invented the wheel, the first
big breakthrough, but women will let the wheels of their
contrivances squeak and squeak until any man within hearing
distance is driven to distraction. The solution to the problem
is so simple, but even if the man, in desperation, gets a can of
oil he knows it is no use giving it to the woman because she
wouldn't have the least idea where to apply it.

As is well known even the mechanics of something as simple as a tube of toothpaste are beyond her comprehension. A
man of course squeezes it from the bottom, knowing that
that is the logical way to get the maximum thrust from the
outlet. But with women it's plonk with the thumb on the
middle of the tube and no matter how often and how painstakingly her husband explains to her that she is thereby building up problems for herself later in the life of the tube, she
will continue in her impractical way.

It is often put that the fact that women are impractical is
very much of their own doing. As soon as a girl is old enough
to get a good hold on something, her mother puts a doll into
her hands. She is soon given a little baby carriage just like

mummy's, is shown how to dress up a doll, or a real baby if one happens to be handy. Sewing, knitting, cooking—she is channeled into all the feminine pursuits. She is brainwashed. All her conditioning dins into her: "You're a girl, see. Just get that straight."

The importance of conditioning in youth is borne out by the story of Alec Templeton, the blind pianist. He was born blind and his parents decided that they would not tell him that he was different from any other boy or girl. He was treated normally. His mother, for instance, would ask him to go upstairs and fetch something from her room and as he felt his way up the stairs and sought out by touch the spool of thread or whatever it was, he thought that this was the way every other boy and girl did things. He was perfectly adjusted, with no sense of self-pity. Then one day a woman visiting the family said: "You poor little blind boy." And he asked: "What does 'blind' mean?"

Frequently the view is expressed that it would be an interesting experiment if a group of girls in isolation could be brought up with hammer and nails instead of dolls, given chemistry sets and construction kits instead of dress patterns and pots and pans. A spokeswoman for the Toy Manufacturers Association said recently: "If only parents would give little girls, instead of dolls, blocks to play with, which is what they *want* to play with." Nobody, however, has yet found it practical to isolate a batch of girls on a desert island or some such place and undertake the boys' toys experiment. Would females, in fact, grow up conditioned to be as practical and inventive as men?

One doubts it, considering the fact that since the emancipation which was supposed to give them a measure of freedom to express themselves there have been so many things developed which women could and should have done something about and haven't. The typewriter is a perfect example.

The typewriter, with which women are far more closely associated than men, is an inefficient machine, and the more it is "improved" the more inefficient it gets. (Don't say that the *electric* typewriter is a great step forward! The world records for speed-typing reveal the amazing fact that the champion on an electric typewriter manages to be only two words per minute faster than the champion on the good old-fashioned manual machine. All that time, effort, and money invested in something that gets only two more words per minute!)

The so-called improvements to the typewriter have clearly been evolved by men who are not called upon to use it day in day out, otherwise they would know what extra, annoying work they have made for the girls at the machines. Erasing is the main focus of the unnecessary difficulties they have built into the modern machine.

In the old days the hinged bar which drops down to hold the paper firmly to the roller used to swing back and forth *toward* the typist. That was fine. It meant that when you wanted to undertake some erasures on your top copy and the carbons you could pull it toward you, out of the way, leaving lots of room for your activities. Now, however, they've "improved" that by having the bar swing away from you to a position which makes it impossible to get straight at the pages and carbons. You have to thread them all toward you under the bar, do your erasures, assemble them again and then thread them back under the back. If you don't know what this is all about, believe me, every stenographer does. It is an irritating waste of time and effort, which didn't exist until the improvers got to work on the typewriter.

Having introduced that annoying modification, they then decided to have the machine looking really slick by incorporating a piece of plastic on each side of the machine where the keys hit the paper. I haven't yet found anybody who can tell me what these two bits of plastic are for. Nearest I got was somebody telling me: "Oh, they're for taking off because they get in the way." You see, they prevent you from getting your eraser at what you want to erase.

But so beautifully designed is the modern machine that even if you take them off it is almost a certainty that it's not

going to do you any good. You still can't get your eraser to
what you want to rub out. Having created this problem,
where none existed before, the designers solved it brilliantly
by incorporating a platform above and behind the roller.
With a twirl of the roller you move the page up so that the
error you have made is get-atable. Having rubbed it out, you
twirl the roller back and continue typing. This is great—except that it doesn't work when you are approaching the bottom of the page. In that situation the paper comes right out
of the machine and you have all the trouble of replacing it in
precisely the right position. And when you are working with
carbons, this is quite impossible. Stenographers all over the
world are furious about this, day after day.

If only women would become inventive and do something
which the girls who use typewriters would really appreciate.
Why not incorporate a counter which would tell you how
many lines you have typed as you go down the page? This
would be of immense help to anyone who has to do a big job
of thousands of words, like the manuscript of a book, say, or
a long report. Supposing she has decided to do twenty-five
lines to the page, how does the typist know automatically
when she has done the required twenty-five? She doesn't. She
has to work out some laborious system of her own for this
sort of thing. A line counter built into the machine would
save her an enormous amount of time.

So, there are numerous things about just that one machine,
the typewriter, which women could do something about, if
they had an inventive bent. They cannot make the excuse
that they have come late to the field of inventing and there is
nothing much left to invent. Why doesn't some woman come
up with the idea that will solve the problem which the manufacturers of cellophane tape have been trying desperately to
solve: how to obviate the tedious scraping along a roll of
cellophane tape with your fingernail trying to get at the
stuck-down end of it. If some woman would come up with a
simple, effective solution to that bugaboo, she could just sit
back and watch her fortune in royalties roll in.

And the microphone, that thing which man, the great inventor, has made a complete hash of. Here we are, into the 1970's, and we are still presented with the unsightly picture on television of an interviewer shoving a hand mike in front of the interviewee's mouth, back to his own mouth, then back to the interviewee. Even worse, a female entertainer spends hundreds of dollars on a superb dress, accessories, makeup, and hairdo, and completely disrupting our view of how expensively terrific she looks is an ugly microphone on a stand with a wire dangling from it. Some progress has been made with "directional mikes" but why doesn't some woman invent a really efficient one that can be aimed, off camera, in any circumstances, at the person concerned—something which men have proved themselves incapable of achieving.

Over to you, girls.

NOVELISTS

Men	*Women*
Defoe	Jane Austen
Fielding	The Brontës
Trollope	Mrs. Gaskell
Thackeray	George Eliot
Dickens	Daphne du Maurier
Galsworthy	Nancy Mitford
Henry James	Muriel Spark
Maugham	Colette
Conrad	Sagan
Thomas Hardy	Vicki Baum
Herman Melville	Willa Cather
Mark Twain	Edith Wharton
Steinbeck	Edna Ferber
Hemingway	Pearl S. Buck
Faulkner	Carson McCullers
Marquand	Mary McCarthy
Capote	Edna O'Brien

Thomas Mann
Rabelais
Flaubert
Zola
Turgenev
Tolstoy
Dostoevsky
Stendhal
Victor Hugo
Balzac
Albert Camus
Evelyn Waugh
George Orwell
Priestley
Harold Robbins
Conan Doyle
Simenon
Raymond Chandler
Ian Fleming
etc., etc.

Iris Murdoch
Agatha Christie
Dorothy L. Sayers
Virginia Woolf
Gertrude Stein
Louisa Mae Alcott

The novel is the sole field in which women have shown any indication of being capable of holding their own with men. The writing of fiction has of course always been and still is dominated by men. This is borne out by a study of the complete stock list of NAL paperbacks, which reveals these figures:

NOVELS

	By men	By women
General list	148	35
Mysteries	76	1
Classics	125	13
Totals	349	49

In Somerset Maugham's *Ten Greatest Novels of the World*, eight are by men and two (*Pride and Prejudice* and *Wuthering Heights*), by women.

However, this is a very creditable showing on the part of women, in sharp contrast to the fact that one racks one's brains in vain trying to think of a *single* woman philosopher, say, or composer, or mathematician.

Feminists will point to this female success with the novel as a prime example of how women, given equal opportunity, can be as good as men. Virtually all novels, by men or women, are written in the home. Men could exert restrictive pressures on women in the outside world and prevent them from entering, let alone getting anywhere, in the fields of business, industry, science, law, and so on. But in the home they couldn't stop women filling exercise books with fiction. And so, on an equal footing with male writers, such women as Jane Austen, the Brontë sisters, and George Eliot emerged as novelists of equal stature with male contemporaries such as Thackeray, Trollope, and Dickens.

But this argument collapses when you think of all the other things women could have done in the home, away from masculine restrictive practices. They could have sat down at the old spinet or the harpsichord and done some composing. But where are the women composers? They could have filled their notebooks with philosophic thoughts or mathematical propositions. But where are the women philosophers and mathematicians? Or, to keep it in the writing field, why have they not flourished as poets and playwrights as well as novelists, since the quiet of the home is just as conducive to evolving poems and plays.

No. It is not valid to say that the sole reason women have been able to succeed with the novel is because they have had equality of opportunity and to infer from that that they could have done just as well in other spheres under the same circumstances.

The simple fact is that they have the sensitivity to react to the human emotions which are the raw material of novels and a proclivity for indulging in daydreams and weaving fantasies, some of which are capable of standing up to readership by the general public. And the novel is the ideal place to give rein to this, since it is a sufficiently loose form of composition, unlike poetry and drama, where one has to grapple in the first case with the structures of meter and rhyme and in the latter with the mechanics of stagecraft. Of all forms of writing, the novel is the nearest to merely talking on paper, and talking of course is a feminine specialty.

Women, being subjective, of course always write about themselves. Their protagonist is almost without exception a female, like as not a girl growing up, physically and/or mentally, *i.e.*, autobiographical. As one woman admitted to me: "Women write about what has happened to them, what will happen to them and what they hope will happen to them." Men will choose a male or female as their protagonist. One can reel off the titles of dozens of novels by men of which the central character is a woman: *Nana, Anna Karenina, Madame Bovary, Tess of the d'Urbervilles, Sylvia Scarlett, Lady Chatterley's Lover*, Maugham's *Theatre*, Isherwood's *I Am a Camera*, Capote's *Breakfast at Tiffany's*, etc. And if one would read the best story of a girl growing up, read *Kitty Foyle*, by Christopher Morley, of which it has been said exasperatedly by women, "How could a man know so much about what goes on in a girl's mind?"

There is no equivalent list of famous novels by women with male protagonists. The reason is contained in one simple word: research.

Women, even the modern ones, have never given any broad indication of being able to write the *researched* novel. They write about what is readily at hand. Their novels are about *me* growing up ("Boys were beginning to *notice*"), *me* coming to the big city from the little old home town and getting involved with a married man ("We can't go on meeting this way in the back row at the Paramount . . ."), *me* living in a dreary rooming house ("I was horrified to see my underwear was still hanging up to dry when Philip arrived"), love among the filing cabinets at the office, *me* coping with the kids and grappling with female contraception ("She was sitting there on the floor with the accoutrements and the instruction leaflet and she was crying because she could not manage them"), the Other Woman, divorce, menopause, abortion—the whole feminine syndrome rendered into fiction.

The subjectivity of women does not allow them to stand off from themselves and put themselves in other people's shoes. A male author will get an idea for a novel and spend countless weeks, months, finding out how, say, a department store or a real estate office functions, so that he can write with authenticity about that unfamiliar background. He will spend endless time in public libraries going through newspaper clippings. He will journey to a hitherto unknown locale so that he can get inside the minds of people—male and female—who bear no relationship whatsoever to the life he leads but whom he feels will make a good story. A woman novelist merely writes about her own life and its running mate, her dream life.

One must except a book such as *The Fountainhead* by Ayn Rand, one of the most powerfully written *researched* novels of the postwar era, but it is merely a ray of hope among those such as Mary McCarthy's *The Group* and Jacqueline Susann's *Valley of the Dolls*, which epitomize the "Life Among Us Women" type of novel.

It is possible to open up a novel, read a few passages, and say at once whether it is was written by a man or a woman because women are predominantly subjective writers.

Novels by women have certain predictable characteristics, some or all of which show themselves before many pages have gone by, even novels by the "modern" woman writer of whom it is said "she writes like a man."

If male characters in the book have high-sounding names like Sebastian Lovegrove, Gaylord Kirkland, and Peregrine Cavendish you can bet your last dime it's by a woman. When women daydream over the kitchen sink about encountering a devastatingly handsome, unattached man while on a stroll along that beach at Cape Cod he is always called something like Sebastian Lovegrove, never Bert Plum. In this regard it is interesting that Sophia Loren might be thought to have got herself a man with a name which a woman novelist would use as connoting an intriguing Latin Lover. But in fact Carlo Ponti is Italian for Charlie Bridges.

Ever since writers were freed from the Victorian convention that all that women had was an "upper part" of the body and you could call a breast a breast, women novelists have been going on about this thing about their young heroine suddenly realizing that expansion is well under way. Over and over again we have had the scene with the girl in her bedroom, door locked, looking at her naked form in a mirror —front *and* side view—coming to the joyous conclusion that, "Today I am a woman!" Or, if our girl is the introverted type, being terribly self-conscious about it and trying to flatten them down to camouflage her silhouette. This mirror sequence has become such a cliché of women's novels that more than one authoress has felt prompted to freshen it up a bit by giving it a new twist. In one of her recent books a leading woman novelist had the brilliant idea of having her heroine catch sight of her naked reflection in the wet tiled floor of her cubicle at the school swimming pool while drying herself:

"Good God," she cried out, "just look at me, how weird I look from underneath" . . . She had been truly moved by herself, by her own watery image, her grotesquely elongated legs, her tapering waist, and above all by the undersides of her breasts, never seen before . . . She stood there and stared at herself . . . a wet statue, a statue in water, a Venus rising from the sea, with veined marble globes for breasts. She had never expected to be beautiful, and she was startled to see how nearly she approached a kind of beauty.

This bust observation sequence, whether in a mirror or as a watery image, is something which has no counterpart in novels by men. I cannot think of a single novel by a man which has its young hero standing naked in front of a mirror and saying: "Good heavens, my balls have dropped."

Even a "modern" such as Margaret Drabble, acclaimed in England as among the best new modern novelists, cannot resist the temptation to trot out the tired old scene. In her novel about herself called *Jerusalem the Golden*, we learn that heroine Clara "developed young, to the astonishment of her contemporaries" and what excitement there was in the school changing room when the discovery was made! Not being the introverted type, Clara gave her upperworks their full freedom and found that her "possession of big breasts" caused her to be accepted into the smartest clique at the school when formerly she had been ignored. "She was gratified by this change of front," wrote Miss Drabble, which is a neat turn of phrase and the only indication I have yet been able to detect in her writing, as with the other earnest authoresses, that she has a sense of humor, even if unintentional.

You can be sure that any novel by a woman will miss no opportunity to go into great detail about that feminine obsession—clothes. The plot must wait while considerable yardage is devoted to descriptions of flared skirts, embossed georgette, filigree lace, cowl collars, ruching, and floral tulle. And it is a safe bet that in at least one of her novels a woman writer will trot out that other tired old scene about the young heroine suffering agonies because she goes to her first formal dance not in a nice new party frock of her own but in one of her sister's hand-me-downs.

Nor can women novelists resist the temptation to dwell on another of their preoccupations—flowers. A male novelist will write: "She walked through the garden to the river." But not your woman novelist. With her it is "She walked along the gravel path fringed by azaleas, larkspurs, antirrhinum, hyacinths, love-in-a-mist and the sweet smelling saxifraga." Which does nothing whatsoever to further the plot.

If a woman novelist doesn't start her book with a description of dawn—"The steely fingers of dawn were entwining themselves in the quaint cobbled streets and old-world fishermen's cottages of Driftwood-on-Sea when Norsia awoke . . ."

—you can be sure she will get around to it somewhere along the line. *And* sunset. Women novelists love describing dawns and sunsets in great detail. A woman writer will dwell for a page and a half on the sinking of the sun in the western sky as though she were the only person in the world who had ever seen a sunset. The only fresh thing I know worth writing about sunsets is this intriguing fact: observe a sunset upside down and it's sensational. By this I mean turn your head down and around so that you're looking at the skyline with the sky below instead of above the horizon. At once all the colors of the sunset are brilliantly intensified. Reason: When you, in effect, turn the view upside down your eye no longer identifies trees, houses, and so on; the whole thing becomes just a pattern and your vision is free to make the most of the coloring.

Sex, which has never been a restraining influence on male novelists, gives female authors great cause for worry. There is a little group of modern women novelists who have decided to be very modern as far as sex is concerned and the result invariably makes embarrassing, if not laughable, reading.

This, for example:

He stepped towards her and took her in his arms . . . and pushed her very slightly to one side, so that her head was against the wall, so that they were in a small wedge of the kitchen and could not be seen from the other room. Then he kissed her. She returned his kiss with ardour and held on to him tightly; he was hot, and his body under his shirt felt very hard. He continued to kiss her, and to press against her.

When he let her go, they both glanced once more nervously at the other room, and then he took her hand, and lifted it up, and kissed it, on the palm, and said, [Wait for it!] "I'll carry the tray, if you take the packet of digestive biscuits."

And another example:

When they reached his office . . . they lay there upon the mock parquet tiles, lit by the band of fluorescent light, their heads in the space under his desk, staring upwards together, finally, at the unknown underside of the desk, amidst the smell of polish, and the unswept cigarette ash of the day, and the small round paper punchings from his secretary's filing activities. Clara's hair, shortly, was as full of paper punchings, as of confetti. [Symbolism.]

After a while, he said,

"Just think, just think, if you hadn't come." [Needs re-writing.]

"I can't imagine," she said, sitting up and staring down at him, "how you could think I might not come. [Rewrite.] How could I ever have stayed away from you? You must be the most beautiful person that I ever saw in my whole life. I would have been mad to have stayed away."

"And you still see it that way?" he said, still lying flat, his arms crossed comfortably behind his head.

"Why should I not?" she said. "It was very nice, it's been very nice. I wouldn't have missed it, not for anything."

And they stared at each other, reflective, hopeful, satisfied.

Then she fished her brown jersey out of the wastepaper basket, where she had dropped it, and started to get dressed again.

Oh, no! And these samples are from an authoress publi cized as "one of the most able and exciting young British novelists writing today."

But apart from these bold, sex-on-the-office-floor moderns, women novelists are uniform in getting slightly panicky when sex rears its lovely head. They don't know quite how to handle it. They find it very tricky for the simple reason that they are terribly conscious that if they go into too much detail they will reveal just how naive they are about sex. But over the years they have evolved a technique for getting around the whole problem. They bring on the old asterisks. This sort of thing:

Lying under the iridescent laburnum, amidst Spring's earliest hint of wild flowers, Norsia, in her sequined taffeta romper dress, could feel Eliot's hot breath on her cheek. This was it, she knew within herself. Slowly, almost imperceptibly, his lips drew closer to hers . . .

*   *   *

Next morning Norsia was up with the larks and her heart was singing as lustily as they.

This overcomes the difficulty quite neatly. And it will be observed that our "modern" up above, although no doubt eschewing asterisks on the score that they are old-fashioned, nevertheless does precisely the same thing by the simple use of the one word "finally," a useful contrivance for leapfrogging over the sex scene.

But I think my favorite cliché of the woman's novel is the Summarizing Paragraph. This final paragraph is designed to comfort the reader, to leave the reader with the feeling that there is Hope. The authoress gives a quick recap of the situation, through the thoughts of the heroine. Her mother is dying. She is pregnant by a married man. She has just learned that her favorite brother has fallen to his death down an open manhole in Bombay. Her lavatory cistern keeps overflowing.

Then comes the clincher at the end: "But as she turned away from the window aglow with the myriad hues of sunset to stir the baked beans, an inward smile, a sort of radiance suffused her face. *She knew everything was going to be all right.*"

When women stop writing this sort of high-flown reportage of their personal hopes, dreams and setbacks, and write instead researched novels about people outside their own limited sphere the quality of their novels will start to measure up to the quantity of their output.

PHILOSOPHERS

Men	Women
Socrates	?
Plato	
Diogenes	
Confucius	
Spinoza	
Kant	
Schopenhauer	
Nietzsche	
Burke	
Epicurus	
Benjamin Franklin	
Thoreau	
Diderot	
Voltaire	
Locke	
Hobbes	
Mill	
etc., etc.	

There are no women philosophers. Women have no accept-able excuse for this state of affairs. They cannot argue that they were held back in this field by men's restrictive practices as in medicine, law, and so on. As with the novel, in which we have seen they have made a considerable contribution, the field of philosophy has been wide open to them. There is no great trick to being a philosopher. All you need to do is read some books, observe humanity around you and then, armed with pencil and notebook, go off and sit under a tree and think. Whether you will be a good philosopher is another matter, but the point is that those are the simple tools of the trade and available to women and men alike.

Why, then, have women proved themselves quite incapable of producing a Spinoza, Nietzsche, or John Stuart Mill? The reason is basic to the makeup of women. Women, as we shall see in more detail, are subjective; men are objective. A man can go off by himself and ponder the question "Why do we exist?" and come up with some penetrating, thought-provoking answers. If a woman goes off and sits under a tree the sort of question she is most likely to put to herself is: "Young Johnnie is still wetting the bed at nine years of age—is it my fault?"

RELIGIOUS REPORTERS

Men	Women
Matthew	?
Mark	
Luke	
John	
etc., etc.	

It speaks for itself. Apparently no women were there taking notes. It would have been interesting to have been able to read a feminine version of the whole thing.

SPORTS

It would be pointless to list male sports stars and see how women stack up against them. They don't. No women, individually or as a team, have ever been capable of beating or even coming anywhere near equaling men at any sport.

Quick like a fox some feminist would interpose triumphantly: "What about show jumping!" All right, so a woman has on occasion proved that her horse is better at maneuvering a series of hurdles than the horse of some man. But let's get on to our own two feet.

In numerous spheres women may justifiably argue that they have been discriminated against, have not had equal opportunity with men. But this certainly cannot be put forward as an explanation for their pitiful showing in sports. There *has* been discrimination against the Negro in this field. One need not enlarge here on what is still going on in South Africa. But it is interesting that a similar sort of thing happened in the United States. In the prewar days, before blacks had full voting rights in America, it was noted by outside observers that Americans were not above using their second-class citizens to help them dominate the world in such sports as track (Eddie Tolan, Jesse Owens, etc.), and boxing (Jack Johnson, Joe Louis, etc.). But for domestic consumption, in pro baseball, no blacks were allowed to participate until 1948 (Jackie Robinson).

But in sports women have never experienced such discrimination. In fact it is a glowing example of their never having had anything to complain about in that regard. For example, long before the United States of America was ever heard of women were full participants in cricket. There still exists the report of a women's match which took place in 1745, "between eleven maids of Bramley and eleven maids of Hambleton" on Gosden Common, Guildford, just outside London. Women have, therefore, been playing competitive cricket for well over two centuries.

Not that it has done them much good, mind you. England has yet to include a woman on their teams which compete with their deadly rival, Australia, in their fight for the trophy known as the Ashes. But that equivalent of baseball's World Series is for men, it could be argued. Nonsense. So keen is the rivalry between England and Australia that you can be sure that if women came up with a real crackerjack cricketer capable of holding her own with the best of men, she'd be called into service for the England team.

But let us turn to a more truly international sport—tennis. The girls have had every chance here. Wimbledon's "world championship" started for men in 1877. The ladies' singles championship was instituted just seven years later. The U.S. men's championship started in 1881 and women got theirs in

1887. So it cannot be said that in tennis, as in all other sports, women have not had a fair crack of the whip, even though in the early days they underwent certain hardships through their desire to maintain the False Front (see Chapter 8). Elizabeth Ryan, nineteen times Wimbledon champion before and after World War I, once said: "There used to be a drying rack in the ladies' changing rooms over which we would hang our clothes at the end of a match. Alongside the dresses it was not unusual to see whalebone corsets, stained with blood in places—evidence of the suffering we cheerfully endured in the name of propriety."

The thing is that in tennis and all other games they have always been given their heads, with full freedom to develop their talents. Over a long period. Mary, Queen of Scots, was a keen golfer.

But the sad fact is that although women today have proved themselves capable of competing on level terms with men for seats in Congress, say, or on the Board of Directors, the idea of their fighting it out with men on level terms on the sports fields is laughable. A woman baseball player facing up to a major league pitcher? St. Winifred's Basketball Babes versus the Harlem Globe Trotters? A young lady bucking the line at the Rose Bowl? It is of course ridiculous, because of the straight biological fact that they are the weaker sex physically. It is obvious that they just haven't the brute strength to meet men head-on or in bodily contact sports. So let's consider them side by side, as in athletics, for example.

Female performances in athletics underline in red ink their complete inadequacy compared to men.

The first shattering fact revealed by the statistics is that any world record in field or track events held by women can be beaten by SCHOOLBOYS. The kindest thing that can be said about how female track stars shape up in action is that they look awkward. If God had meant women to run, He wouldn't have encumbered them the way He did.

And the second interesting thing is that the oft-repeated claim that when it comes to stamina women have it all over men is just so much nonsense. In track events women stop at 1,500 meters. None of your 3,000 meters, 10,000 meters, etc., for them, let alone the cruel 26 miles 385 yards of the marathon.

Even in tennis their famous stamina allows them to carry on that leisurely brand of baseline patball of theirs only for best of three sets, as against men's best of five. And even with the help of men in the mixed doubles they must call a halt after three sets.

Which brings us to one of the most unrealistic aspects of the Women's Liberation movement. Under its tennis nickname of Women's Lob, women have at last found something in the sporting world about which they feel they can raise a rumpus on the score of discrimination—money. At time of writing there is so much going on regarding the fight by a section of the female pro tennis players for equality with men in prize money that if I went into a lot of detail here, it would all be outdated by the time this book appears. So the only comment I would make is that there is a basic fact which nobody seems to bring out. That is that it is right and proper that men get and should continue to get more tennis prize money than women—on the age-old basis that a workman is worthy of his hire. Men, battling out their best-of-five matches for anything up to four hours twenty minutes (Drobney v. Patty, Wimbledon, 1953), provide much more entertainment than the ladies, who can finish off their best-of-threes in half an hour or so. Equal pay for equal work is one thing, but this is just not on.

But one should not be purely derogatory about women in sports. Let us be constructive.

The point is that men excel in sports, which men invented and which women have butted into. Why don't women invent a sport of their own? Heaven alone knows what it would be—the Hop-Splits-and-High-Kick? But at least it would be a sport tailor-made for them physically and mentally. It would be a sport at which they would be paramount and which would free them from the demoralizing feeling of always coming in second to men.

3 THE FEMININE PURSUITS

As mentioned earlier, the staggering thing is that even in the so-called feminine pursuits, spheres in which women naturally would be expected to be far more prominent than men, it is males who dominate. Let us examine this a little more closely in these examples.

CHILD CARE

Men	*Women*
Spock (U.S.A.)	?
Brock (Canada)	
Sir Truby King (New Zealand)	
etc.	

If ever there were a field in which women would be expected to dominate it is in the matter of giving practical advice and evolving regimens for the rearing of children. Yet it is men such as those mentioned above who have achieved international reputations as the great authorities, with Spock's *Baby and Child Care* (over 20,000,000 copies sold), the new mother's bible of course.

Why this should be so, heaven alone knows.

COOKING

All the best restaurants throughout the world—on land and afloat—have chefs. It would be inconceivable to have a wom-

an in charge where food at its best is expected by the pa-
trons.

DRESSMAKING

Men	*Women*
Worth	Chanel
Mainbocher	Schiaparelli
Molyneux	Quant
Dior	
Balmain	
St. Laurent	
Courrèges	
Hartnell	
Cardin	
etc., etc.	

Now here is a field in which one could be certain that women
would naturally dominate—the designing of their beloved
clothes. After all, from the time a girl is only *that* high she is
taught to sew, while boys are instructed in the more manly
pursuits. But as things turn out in later life it is only on the
level of the local seamstress that women do run the show. In
big-time fashion, with but few exceptions, it has long been
men who have been the dominant designers, the pace-setters
for what the well-dressed women of the world will wear.

The socialites on the Park Avenue-Fifth Avenue axis don't
turn to those of their own sex to give them clothes guidance.
They look to the Paris collections of a St. Laurent or a Cour-
règes to dictate each new trend. The Dress Designer to Her
Majesty the Queen of England is not some Jessie Stitchright.
The Queen (no Women's Liberator she, even her private secretary and two assistant private secretaries are men) of course
has a man to design her regal look.

This male influence on fashion permeates through to wom-
en everywhere who want to make an impression with the

clothes they wear. Why is it that they have to get men to do it for them?

One reason is that if fashion were an all-women affair you would get that well-known bitchiness creeping in. Wearing some female-designed creation, a woman would only need to hear some other woman say that it looks *awful* for her immediately to abandon the thing. But if a man has designed it, if she can say with *hauteur* that it is Monsieur Latouche's latest brainchild, well that's different.

Also if women were completely in charge of what their clothes should look like they would be deadly dull. As we shall see, in the matter of sex, women are naive about how to present themselves. And the same thing applies to what they wear. Men bring imagination, a sense of excitement and flair to women's clothes.

Don't think there isn't a good reason why photos in the glossy fashion magazines—any fashion shots for that matter—are almost always taken by men. It is nothing to do with their being able to handle cameras better than women, who are just as capable technically. The simple truth is that they bring a bit of zipperoo to the pictures, make the models and the clothes look exciting. When women design and photograph their own clothes it looks like *haute couture* in Deadwood, South Dakota.

POETRY

Men	*Women*
Horace	Sappho
Homer	Christina Rossetti
Shakespeare	Elizabeth Barrett Browning
Keats	Emily Dickinson
Shelley	
Byron	
Milton	
Browning	

Wordsworth
Coleridge
Yeats
Brooke
Eliot
Spender
Dylan Thomas
Longfellow
Ezra Pound
Robert Frost
Goethe
Verlaine
Baudelaire
etc., etc.

The writing of poetry is so very much a feminine pursuit that at school if a boy is caught by his chums doing it he is likely to be pounded for being a sissy.

Schoolgirls, lovesick maidens, frustrated housewives churn it out by the ream and the mistake so many of them make is that they think somebody else might like to read it. For a number of years I was a magazine editor and one thing I learned, something which became imprinted on my mind, was this: Never run poetry. If an editor does make the mistake of including a poem in an issue he finds himself immediately inundated with contributed verse, 90 percent of it from women, practically all of it rubbish. It makes an editor's life much easier just not to run any poetry. When a woman is sitting across from him at his desk and starts saying, "Just by chance I happen to have with me . . . ," you can be pretty darn sure it's a poem she has written and quick as a flash he can call a halt by saying, "Sorry, we don't carry any poetry." This can mean that an editor may miss out on the occasional good poem (useful for plugging up a hole in a page) but on balance it is much better abruptly to ward off the female versifiers.

Those who run record-request programs on radio are sometimes a bit lax in this regard and let through—you know the type of thing:

> *If this record for me you play,*
> *It will surely make my day.*

That epitomizes the sort of stuff women turn out when they are under the impression that they are writing poetry, typified by the inverted phraseology and *always* each line ending with a single-word rhyme. In all justice they can point to the songs of the Beatles and say that without exception *they* rhyme single-syllable words, with the "sad-glad" pair as in:

> *I used to feel so glad*
> *But now I feel so sad*

being the ever-recurring partners. One can only admit that the splendid songs of Lennon and McCartney are somewhat marred by this fault, which could be easily rectified if they got hold of the sort of rhyming dictionary (the one published by Routledge & Kegan Paul, Ltd. is very good) which has been of such help to such brilliant rhymsters as Cole Porter, Oscar Hammerstein II, and Noel Coward.

But to return to our poetesses. The point one would make is that rarely in any other field can such huge output be seen to produce so little of value.

Somebody once made the observation that when a piece of verse starts with "And when . . ." it is by a major poet and when it ends with ". . . and how," you may be sure that it is by a minor poet. It is perhaps unfair to stand in judgment on the women mentioned above because they are very definitely in the minor leagues. Let us turn to the "And When" poets and ask ourselves why it is that when women enter the professional ranks, as it were, their poetry just cannot stand comparison with that produced by men?

The answer, sad to say, lies in an aspect of women which I am afraid is going to crop up again and again in this attempt I am making to analyze what makes women tick.

In another context I have quoted the Winston Dictionary's example of the application of the word "subjectivity": "The *subjectivity* of Mrs. Browning as shown in her sonnets." As long as women continue to be subjective beings, unable to stand off from things and view them objectively, they will continue to write poems about this own personal little world, my blighted love, my heavy heart, my this, my that, instead of poems of stature and more lasting worth.

SHORTHAND

Men	Women
Pitman	?
Gregg	

SINGING SOPRANO

The all-time biggest selling phonograph record in this field is *O For the Wings of a Dove* sung by Ernest Lough—a BOY soprano.

TALKING

Men	Women
Socrates	?
Dr. Johnson	
Oscar Wilde	
Lord Birkenhead	
Winston Churchill	
Clarence Darrow	

Billy Graham
Edward R. Murrow
Walter Cronkite
Jack Paar
David Frost
etc., etc.

Women do much more talking than men. But never to such effect. There is no female equivalent of the broad sweep of great male talkers. The spellbinders of the forums of Athens and Rome. Boswell in the eighteenth-century London coffee-houses jotting down everything the great conversationalist said. The Wilde witticisms of café society. The great orators. Churchill versus the two evil ones and winning out over them, to become by far the most quoted of modern orators. The evangelists, the One who started it all not listed above because everybody knows that He was the man with the greatest ability to sway people with words who ever lived. The great legal advocates. The men of radio. And now television's news analysts, commentators, narrators, and adroit exponents of the TV talk show.

We have come a long way from Socrates to David Frost. Which is not intended at all to be a frivolous comment. Each age makes its particular calls on those expert at the use of the spoken word and at this moment in time there happen to be millions of people, from Seattle to Brisbane, from Glasgow to Dunedin, who want to listen hour after hour to the Talk Show.

Women can be forgiven for not coming up with a Socrates, a Churchill, or a Clarence Darrow, since they can no doubt put up numerous excuses, such as not being allowed to, through being held down by men. But there would seem to be no excuse whatsoever for being completely secondary when it comes to something which would clearly appear to be right up their street—transferring their great facility for chitchat to entertainment for the viewing millions. Sure they talk away by the hour on TV for women viewers and children. But why is it that men dominate the talk show for the mass audience, who are more than grateful that they do?

There are sound reasons for this.

Earlier we mentioned the "How Am I Doing?" complex, the inherent desire of women to know what sort of impression they are making. This is a root cause of their not making good television interviewers. They will come on the TV screen all dolled up, with a new hair creation just for the occasion, etc., and all the time the viewer is conscious that they are conscious of the image they are projecting ("Maybe I shouldn't have worn this choker, maybe it wobbles up and down as I speak . . ."). Their minds are not 100 percent on the job at hand—to get the best possible interview out of their guest. Men are not burdened with such worries. David Frost cares not a whit about his clothes. He has about as much dress sense as a stripper. Good. He is free to concentrate on the job.

The subjectivity of women (What will people think of *me*?) extends beyond just their physical appearance when locked in debate with a stimulating TV guest. They can be thrown off stride so easily. Some male guest only needs to say something outlandlish like "Wet dreams don't worry me, I find you meet a much better type of girl," and at once the interviewess is covered with confusion, dithers, flaps, and she compounds it all by chiding herself with what a terrible impression she's making, and it all gets worse and worse as she tries to flounder her way out of her embarrassment. Men play on this and know that if they are getting the worst of things from a woman interviewer it is the easiest thing in the world to throw something at her which will make her reveal herself as predictably feminine. The essence of the good interviewer is never to be nonplussed, and men are natural experts at this. They have tricks, you know, to fall back on. For example, if a guest does say something that shows you in a bad light, immediately turn to the studio audience and say: "Well, really!" The audience is there because they think the interviewer is great and can be relied upon to side with him, so the producer sees to it that the camera lingers on the audience reaction on behalf of the interviewer against the recalcitrant guest. Women, too busy flapping, lack the objective expertise to get themselves out of a jam with such a trick. Female viewers in particular are embarrassed because they see their own sex being held up to ridicule when it behaves in this typically feminine way.

If all that were not enough to make the general public much prefer Masters of Ceremonies to Mistresses of Ceremonies, there is that final consideration—women's voices, the unavoidable stumbling block to their getting anywhere of importance not only in the Talk Show world but as newscasters, commentators, and so on. The ear finds it hard to take the higher pitch of the female voice over any length of time. It is not without good reason that in a symphony orchestra the man who plays the double bass gets much more work to do than does the piccolo player.

TYPING

On October 22, 1923, the world's typing record for wordage per hour on a standard machine was established at a rate of 147 errorless words per minute. That means that this entire book could be typed out in a mere ten hours. This wizard of the typing keyboard was of course a man, American, Albert Tangora.

4 THE FOUR STOCK ANSWERS

When one points out to a woman how far feminine achievement lags behind what men have done, one can be sure that she will come back with one of four stock rejoinders—if not all four of them, in a gushing rush.

These are the four:

1. Women have always been held down by men.
2. Behind every successful man is a woman.
3. Men can't have babies.
4. What about Madame Curie!

As regards stock answer No. 1, it is just not a valid argument that from the time cavemen dragged women around by the hair until the wife and daughters of the Victorian master of the house quailed before his mastery, women were given absolutely no chance in a male-dominated world. Granted business concerns would not consider them except as underlings, and there was a similar closed-shop attitude in the medical profession, law, and other spheres requiring qualifications they were not allowed to attain. But there have always been plenty of fields open to them.

When Da Vinci doodled until he came up with designs for a helicopter away ahead of time, any woman was free to have done the same thing. Pencil and paper have always been available to everybody, regardless of sex. Brahms used to go for a walk in the woods and come back with the first movement of a symphony worked out ready to put down on paper. There has never been a closed shop against women working out in

their minds musical themes and their development. For num-
berless years women have gone off to foreign parts, Florence
Nightingale style, as nurses and missionaries. There was never
anything to prevent them, once there, from doing a spot of
exploration and discovering a new continent or even a fair-
sized waterfall. That well-known greeting could just as easily
have been "Daphne Livingstone, I presume!"

But no, women allowed themselves to be subjugated. They
had neither the initiative nor drive to break out. Through
history many men, too, have been similarly shackled—by
such things as poverty, prejudice, and physical disability—and
it has not stopped their achievements. Poverty—Mozart, as
just one example, dancing gavottes with his wife in his garret
to keep warm because they could not afford fuel. Prejudice—
Pasteur carrying on a running battle with officialdom, which
said he hadn't the necessary qualifications to do the great
work he was doing. Physical disability—Roosevelt, polio victim, being one of the most active, greatest statesman at a
most crucial period of the world's history. The expression,
"You can't keep a good man down" has clearly had a purely
male connotation. History shows that you *can* keep a good
woman down. For the simple reason that it is her function to
be subordinate.

In 1920 she tried to prove otherwise. I pick that year
because it is a very convenient date. It was then that American women started voting and very neatly it is half a century
ago. Getting the vote was like getting the first olive out of the
bottle—when you manage to get that one out, the others
come easily. Following on from their getting the franchise all
sorts of other male-locked doors opened up for them. Today,
apart from some very few holdouts, there are not many
spheres of endeavor that are closed tightly against women.

So . . . for the past half century it has not been true to say
that women have been completely held down by men, not
given any chance at all.

But what have they done with their new-found opportunities?

The fact that they have been voting for fifty years has made no discernible difference whatsoever in the way we have been governed.

Women like to tell of the drastic changes they would make if they were running the show. Not the least of these is the matter of war. "If women ran governments," they say over and over again, "there would be no more wars." On the evidence of women disputing possession of a bargain at a Gimbel's sale I don't find it easy to go along with that claim. I find it even more difficult to bring credence to it when I bear in mind that when the Israelis went to war against Egypt in 1967 their head of state was Mrs. Meir, and that Mrs. Gandhi was India's head of state during that country's 1971 conflict with Pakistan.

Putting that aside as irrelevant, the point is that it would be the easiest thing in the world for women to run our government if they really wanted to. They could do it by sheer weight of numbers. In practically every country in which they have the franchise they outnumber men. A national Women's Party, with all their voters getting behind each candidate, could railroad themselves into Congress with a huge majority. They could take over, and men could do nothing about it.

It is a frightening thought. But fortunately women have not the organizing ability to bring off such a coup. The only thing the average woman does with her vote is to say to her husband, boyfriend, or father: "Who do I vote for?"

And there is only one other comment one need make on this oft-repeated excuse of women being held down by men.

In the half century since women became emancipated many brand new fields have opened up. Women have started from scratch alongside men in the whole new world of radio, talking pictures, television, detergents, ballpoint pens, synthetic fibers, drip-dry fabrics, frozen foods, the Pill, jet aircraft, penicillin, insulin, radar, zippers, transistors, paper tissues, plastics, tampons, computers, atomic energy, etc., etc.

No woman, of course, invented any of these things. That goes without saying. But accepting the fact that in the last half century these and so many other new things have become part of our life, what have women done about them, now that they are on an equal footing with men to develop, improve, and otherwise shape the course of these modern boons and so-called boons to society? Nothing that even the most ardent feminist can point to. No woman has even got sufficiently infuriated when trying to iron a blouse made of the new polyesters to develop a new synthetic fiber which you *can* iron like good old silk or cotton.

As regards stock answer No. 2—behind every successful man there is a woman. This is about as self-evident as saying that every baby has a mother. Just as true is the fact that behind every *unsuccessful* man there is a woman. In truth there are far more women behind unsuccessful men than successful ones.

If this needs explanation, every aspiring man may be said to have a woman behind him, be it wife, mistress, girl friend, or mother. These females are naturally interested in his being a success. But there is not a great deal of room at the top. Of every one hundred men, let us say that ten become successful, which may be somewhat generous when one considers the huge proportion of wage slaves to bosses. However, with that as a rough yardstick it is obvious that the vast majority of women are backing losers.

For feminists to point with pride to one of the small proportion of successful men and infer that it is that devoted wife by his side to whom the credit must go is a specious bit of female self-congratulation. It completely overlooks the far greater proportion of wives standing beside husbands who have never got anywhere despite those wives giving them the same sort of support, encouragement, solace, and devotion as the successful ones got.

Another interesting point about this matter of "behind

every successful man there is a woman" is that, as Britain's
Professor Joad would have put it, "it all depends what you
mean by success."

I shall quote just one example to make my point. You can
probably think of numerous others yourself.

Dr. M. was a young doctor from Colorado who went east
because that is where the impressive degrees are. He got
through with flying colors and was all set for a career in New
York, with all its rewards, financial as well as reputation and
stature. I sat back ready to watch his climb to the top, for his
associates were unstinting in their estimate of his brilliance.
Then his wife dragged him back to Colorado.

I did not need to ask Dr. M. what her motives were in
doing this. Her arguments would be: We have your and my
family there, we have all our friends there, with the wonderful qualifications you have now you'll easily be able to get a
marvelous job at such-and-such a hospital, we'll have security
rather than having to battle your way against the fierce competition in New York and (although she would not express
this in words to him) "I'll be really big stuff locally as the
wife of the successful Dr. M."

All of which came to pass. But is he successful? Not in his
own eyes. He did not achieve his goal. He did not even try to
and fail, which would at least have been keeping faith with
himself. Instead, he lowered his sights to please his wife. And
while she dons the finery which will so impress the locals at
the function they are going to, he sits and thinks to himself,
"If only . . ."

In all such cases, which are innumerable, the wife is happy.
Or thinks she is. She knows nothing of the real sort of happiness enjoyed by the wife who is content to let her husband
persevere with what he has set his heart on. Just as in sex,
where the profound satisfaction is to be found in making the
other person happy, the wife who supports rather than deflects her husband's ambition finds the true, far more lasting
type of happiness—reflected happiness.

Stock answer No. 3—men can't have babies. If having a baby were a solo achievement it would indeed be something very wonderful. Women could decide just when they would have each child; there would be no such thing as unwanted babies. The Pope would not need to devote so much time and thought to pronouncements on the subject. But of course it is not how things are. Women are entirely dependent on men as far as procreation is concerned. The decision as to whether or not a woman will have a baby is not hers. She has a baby when her husband, other male associate, or a test-tube donor, is good and ready to give her one. So it is pointless to say that having a baby is an entirely feminine achievement, for it is something a woman can't do by herself, except of course for that isolated and well-known instance.

Stock answer No. 4—what about Madame Curie! In the history of grasping at straws there is nothing to equal this.

Since primitive man rubbed two sticks together and discovered it was possible to make fire, men have never ceased to add chapter after chapter to the enthralling saga of discovery and invention. *Men*, that is. Not women. It is pitiful that women can point with pride to only one solitary contribution from their side—the woman who helped her husband discover radium.

PART TWO

THE
FEMININE
SYNDROME

5 THE GOOD AND BAD IN WOMEN

For the study of the good and bad in women it is unnecessary to study more than one woman. Thus, very wisely, spake American philosopher Ambrose Bierce.

What he meant of course was that invariably contained in every woman is something of all the female characteristics, in contrast to men, who are far more inclined to be "all of a piece"—entirely saintly, for example, or completely a villain. The female evildoer will take time out to display the good feminine qualities of, say, motherly kindliness and warmth of affection. The ardent female church worker in off-duty moments is not above baring her claws at a rival and indulging in malicious gossip.

Dr. Alice Heim, in discussing "The Mediocrity of Women," in her book, *Intelligence and Personality*, wrote that "the top rungs of the achievement ladder are certainly occupied by men and this is very likely a basic psychological fact—as opposed to a sociological one—since the bottom rungs of this and other ladders tend also to be occupied by men." It takes great concentration and singleness of purpose to exploit to the full one's genius as a Beethoven, just as a Capone cannot spare the time for the niceties of masculine behavior. Women not having the singleness of purpose to carry them to the heights of worthy achievement or to the depths of well-organized evil, they must spend most of their time on the middle rungs of the ladder. A man can concentrate to the point of obsession on making himself a great financier or whatever, but if a woman tries it she cannot be just a financier. She

must be a financier *and a woman.* The fact that for the bulk
of her life there is the necessity of menstruating or having a
baby reminds her constantly of her femininity, deflects her
from the full concentration that a man can bring to any
project. The result is that the majority of women take the
much easier course of devoting most of their time to the job
of being a woman and displaying, in varying degrees, all the
facets, ramifications, and complexities of that role.

To list, let alone deal individually with, *all* the female characteristics would be altogether too demanding of space. But
stated in simple terms the spectrum ranges from the good
qualities—the ability to be self-sacrificing, sympathetic, understanding, tender, patient—through such middling qualities
as the tendency to dramatize things, to be impractical and
illogical ("I can't be overdrawn at the bank, I've still got four
checks left in my checkbook."), talkative, nagging, grudge-
holding, vain, obsessed with clothes ("Rachel, you *must* do
something about your appearance, or you'll be mistaken for a
Gentile."), naive about sex (bride to groom in his tub on the
morning after their wedding night: "Is that all we've got
left?")—to the lower levels of being vindictive, bitchy, spiteful, vicious.

In the remainder of this chapter we take a close look at
certain of these feminine qualities. In later chapters the
others cannot help but make themselves manifest.

Self-sacrificing

Without question the finest quality of women is their ability
to be self-sacrificing. They will starve so that their children
are properly fed. They will go in rags in order that they be
warmly clothed. They will do it furtively—the most laudable
form of self-sacrifice, being at pains not to let the person for
whom it is being done know anything about it. Example: A
woman of my acquaintance, when her husband got into money difficulties, said that she must do something to help out,

anything. So she got an early morning job which still left her free each day to look after the family. She told him it was in the mail department of a big organization, sorting out the morning mail. In fact she was working in the building as a paid-by-the-hour cleaning woman.

Men are not nearly as good at being self-sacrificing. Laying down their lives in time of war? All right, so we expose ourselves to that likelihood. But it is most certainly not something we do willingly and uncomplainingly. It is not something we undertake on our own initiative.

Women have in-built willingness to be self-sacrificing. Men are not nearly so inclined that way. Their attitude varies in degree from reluctance to forego their creature comforts for the sake of somebody else to sacrificing other people in order to achieve their ends.

Just think how frequently we see this pattern of behavior: A girl gives up all her own chance in life to devote herself to caring for a disabled mother or to looking after younger brothers and sisters orphaned along with her. In the course of it a brother is thereby afforded the opportunity to make his way in life. And as the years go by and it is too late for any real fulfillment to come her way he is heard to say to her, frequently: "Always I shall remember and be grateful for what you've done for me." Yeah.

How often does it happen the other way around?

In adversity it is the female who is far more ready, more able to cope, and in illustration of this I would tell of a man whom we shall call Dawson.

Dawson was successful in the steel industry. Apart from the war years he had devoted his whole life to knowing about steel and rising to a good position in his firm. Such a good man was he that a rival firm hired him away at a salary which enabled him to have his children at the best schools and maintain a high standard of living. But after barely four years with the new company there was a reshuffle of management and the new Mr. Big decided that Dawson would have to go—to make way for one of his own favorites or because he merely didn't like the way Dawson parted his hair or for any one of a dozen superficial reasons that a man in a seemingly secure job can suddenly find as cause for his being out. The golden handshake Dawson received was not all that golden, since he was virtually a newcomer to that firm. With the commitments in which he had involved himself in his way of life it would not tide him over for very long during his job seeking. But worse than that, he had reached that unemployable age of fifty. It is a cruel axiom of the business world that, although a man may continue in a job at fifty, he cannot start.

I watched Dawson go down and down, become more and more depressed by hearing time and again, "Certainly we know you, Dawson, you're well known in the steel business, but in regard to this particular job we were thinking in terms of—er—a younger man," and that other one, "It is all very well for you to say that you wouldn't mind accepting this lesser job, but we feel you wouldn't really be happy in the work, knowing you have qualifications for something far more important."

I was out of touch with Dawson for a while, during a sojourn abroad, but when I returned I was told, "Everything's all right with him now. Go over to the Havelock and you'll see." The Havelock was a bar and grill and I arrived there to find that Dawson and his wife had been taken on to manage the place with living accommodation above with enough room for their son and daughter when they were home from college.

I was pleased for him and told him so. He glanced at the stack of dirty glasses at the sink under the bar and shrugged. "It is hardly what I have been used to," he said.

I was prompted to say, but didn't, that he was damned lucky to be in worthwhile work. At least two men of his age who frequented the place had seen months stretch into years out of work, with the demoralizing effect of public assistance and loss of self-respect.

In the following weeks I was to observe Dawson at the bar merely going through the motions of his work, standing there looking disgruntled, giving service when he was called upon to do so, making no effort to be affable to customers.

Now here is the interesting point about this.

I had never liked Dawson's wife. I had found her a bore, preoccupied with the trivial, petty, and quick to take offense, especially when she was in her cups, which was frequently. But there at the Havelock she was a changed person. She was attentive, eager to please customers and make them feel welcome. She asked the regulars how their work was going, how was the family—an interest I had not previously noticed her take in other people. Nothing was too much trouble to her. In other words, everything one expects of such a place, well-run. And she was always sober.

What had happened, of course, was what so often—perhaps one should say invariably—happens when a mature man in an apparently secure job suddenly finds himself out of work and unable adequately to support his family. It is his wife who knuckles down to the radically changed circumstances.

While he nurses his injured pride, feels sorry for himself, resentful that the whole world seems against him, she rolls up her sleeves and says now let's get cracking, we've got to do something about getting out of this demoralizing atmosphere. She blossoms or rather, as I am sure was the case with Dawson's wife, she returns to being the alert and active person she was before sliding down into the rut of being a dull housewife with grown children and nothing much to occupy her mind.

There is a very good reason, psychological *and* biological, why this happens. As the psychiatrist, Clifford Thompson, has put it: "Women are born to carry two people." Dawson's wife was in her element when having their children and bringing them up. When they went off to college, she became just the wife of a busy executive—a purely secondary role. But when abruptly her husband was thrown out of his self-contained business world he turned to her for comfort and help, became reliant on her as her children had been. She found herself again with, as it were, a child to look after. And once more she was in her element.

There is, however, an unhappy aspect to this so often to be observed good quality in women. The womanly need to carry two people can become so pressing that a woman can, although she does not consciously set about doing so, create a situation whereby her husband will become reliant upon her. "If I were you I wouldn't stand it any longer, I'd just go straight into the boss in the morning and tell him what he can do with his job." How often that advice, invariably ill-considered, has been given to a man by his wife. And rather than go down in her estimation by appearing spineless, he acts upon it. Presto, he is out of a job and she can once more bring into full play all her motherly instincts.

I have observed this carried to the extent of a woman forcing a man to give up a job in which he was perfectly happy. On a manufactured reason for his leaving his job, she now has him dependent upon her. The key in this case of course was the fact that she had never been able to have children.

The point about all this is that while it is true that a wife can nag a man into doing better for himself, which is the constructive application of nagging, by the same token she can nag him into landing himself and the whole family in an awful jam—for her to step in and take over.

Fortunately, however, that is merely the bad side of the coin, rarely on view compared to the good side.

Intuition

I will go along with certain generalizations about women. That they are better than men at meticulous, finicky work, like threading the bobbins in a textile factory, for example. (Ignore anyone who wants to get awkward about this and says that if they are so great at intricate work, why are there no women watchmakers? That's creative work. Outside their field.) One must agree that it is an outstanding feminine attribute and it is seen to be so when one observes production lines of girls performing the meticulous, finicky, repetitive, monotonous jobs of fitting filaments to electric bulbs, putting whirls on top of chocolates, stitching shoulder straps to bra cups and so on.

But I cannot go along with this thing about women's intuition, simply because it is not seen to have any practical application.

Ashley Montagu, in his book *The Natural Superiority of Women*, says:

The poor blunt average male, when he first encounters woman's intuition, is astonished; it seems to him like magic. After all, he hasn't said a word or in any way indicated to her where he has been and what he has done; yet she knows, and pierces his thin disguises with an appalling certainty! How can anyone keep anything secret from her? Well, just as gamblers will go on believing that they can win in their gambling, so men will continue to believe that they can keep secrets from their wives. But few men have secrets that their wives do not know.

Since Ashley Montagu deals with women's intuition on its lowest level, *i.e.*, a wife catching her husband out in some extramural activity, let us dismiss this with dispatch. *Of course* women are known for this ability to sense that it was dallying with some female rather than work which made her husband home late from the office, plus all the other similar examples of surmising that he is transgressing. But there is no magical intuition about this. The simple truth is that men are made that way, always to be questing, when women have long since decided it is a better idea to settle down to domesticity. Therefore countless opportunities are presented to her to catch her husband out, and from this recurring situation she gets the reputation of being intuitive. She for her part gives her husband few such chances to exercise *his* intuition, so males are not forever being congratulated on their powers of "immediate apprehension by the mind without reasoning," as the dictionaries put it. When she does step off the straight and narrow, her husband is every bit as capable as she is of "piercing her thin disguise with appalling certainty." For example, she is in late from what was billed as an evening out with the girls. She comes in guilt-laden, it is oozing from her every pore, and immediately she dashes to her children and showers them with affection. And her husband, of course, knows that racing through her mind is: "Your Mummy has been terribly naughty. Up to no good in Lancelot Harcourt's penthouse apartment. I'm thoroughly ashamed of myself. My life is with you, my darlings. Will you forgive me if I promise never to do it again, etc., etc." It's a dead giveaway. But her husband doesn't stand by congratulating himself on how the good old male intuition is working in top gear. He just says to himself: "Good for her! She's refreshed her life a bit and now she'll be more content to settle back into her routine."

But to move on to intuition in its broader aspects—Dr. Alice Heim, in the chapter, "The Mediocrity of Women," says:

Woman's famed (or infamous) "intuition" is neither a mystical sixth sense nor is it an utterly unfounded myth. Women's so-called intuitive judgments and perceptions are due not so much to some vague, generalized sensitivity as to acute awareness of a number of small personal details—an awareness that may not even be recognized at the time. Women often have this to a greater extent than men because they are more interested in the small personal details—a change in facial expression, a hesitation in replying, an unusual intonation, a minor alteration in the arrangement of a room. They are interested in the details for their own sake and also for what they signify. Since they are sometimes unwilling to disclose these sources of their opinions, and sometimes unable to do so—and since the interpretations based on these niceties are sometimes correct—the result is often labelled "intuition." The word may be pronounced contemptuously or smugly, according to choice.

If it's all the same with you, Dr. Heim, I'll take "contemptuously."

If women are so adept at reaching accurate conclusions from "sensitivity as to acute awareness of a number of small personal details, change of facial expression, etc.," it should mean that this facility is put to practical use. As with their ability at intricate work, mentioned above, as with their proficiency at coping with young children making them ideal teachers in nursery schools, and so on.

Your Personnel Manager, anyone in charge of hiring people, should invariably be a woman. Her intuition would enable her at once to assess accurately the worth of any candidate for a job, detect immediately the phony, no matter how plausible he might appear to be. But personnel managers aren't invariably women.

Women's intuition should make them great detectives, masters at interrogation. But they are not used in this field. Not even in detective fiction. I do believe Agatha Christie has been trying to give her public a convincing woman sleuth, but it can be truthfully said that we wait in vain for a Sherlockia Holmes.

Until this attribute they are supposed to have is shown to have a practical application, as with women's inherent interest in and sympathy for people making them readily employable as social workers, I think it is safe to say that women's famous intuition is a bit of a fable.

Vanity

Putting aside female missionaries and women so flat-chested that they are acutely embarrassed about it, if you ask any photographer he will tell you that any woman will gladly take her clothes off to be photographed. This includes the most unexpected women such as staid housewives, efficient female executives, and prim schoolteachers. It is all traceable to vanity.

She is having a simple head-and-shoulders taken to send to her mother in Pine Falls, Minn., and the dialogue goes like this:

Photographer: You have very attractive shoulders.
Woman (happily):   Do you think so?
P: *Very* attractive. (*Looking through viewfinder and at pains to indicate that he is interested solely in photographing rare beauty.*) Take your blouse off.
W (taking blouse off):   You really think I have attractive shoulders?
P: They're terrific. (*Changing to disappointed tone.*) No. No.
W: What's wrong?
P: Those shoulder straps—they destroy the beautiful lines from the nape of your neck across the bone structure of your shoulders.
W: I—I suppose they do. (Moves shoulder straps down.)
P: Ah! Oh, that *is* terrific. (*About to click shutter, pauses.*) But wait a minute. Those shoulder straps hanging down. A bit unsightly.
W: Of course. (*Cooperatively warming to this photographic project, she starts tucking shoulder straps out of sight.*)
P: Actually, I think it would be better with the brassiere off.
W: Do you? (*Takes brassiere off.*)
P: Good heavens, what a beautiful figure you have.
W (preening):   Do you really think so?
(*No answer from photographer, too busy recording beautiful figure on film.*)
W: You really think I have a good figure?
P: Listen, I've photographed dozens and dozens of women. *Professional* models. Girls who are in the business for the very reason that they have good figures . . .
W: And you think mine compares with theirs?
P: Compares! More than compares. Believe me . .
W (contentedly):   H'mmmmm.

P: Do you know what we should do?
W: No? What?
P: We should do a full-length shot.
Etc., etc.

Oftentimes, for a photographer it is not so much a matter of whether a woman will take her clothes off. Her vanity can be such that he has the problem of getting her to keep them on.

I remember a number of years ago discovering a movie star, still very active on the big screen, who shall be nameless. I do not wish to appear boastful about "discovering a movie star," because without doubt if I had not unearthed her, she had such drive that she would have made it to the top anyway.

What happened was that at the time I was associate editor of a magazine and happened to notice a shot in a newspaper of this girl with some others at a swimming pool. She struck me as having rare beauty and a photogenic quality which would make her ideal to put on our cover. We contacted the young lady, she would have been eighteen or nineteen then, and a photo session was arranged.

Unfortunately at the last moment our staff photographer, who would normally have done this sort of color picture, came down with flu or something, so I had to call in as substitute one of our photographers whom I shall call Fergus. He was a good man, great on flowers, gardens, and rural scenes. Let him loose on a bunch of chrysanthemums and you knew it would be great, you could see every petal, but he was virtually untried as a glamour photographer. Anyway, we were in a jam so he was doing the shot.

Girl-girl had decided to wear an off-the-shoulder blouse for the occasion and it was certainly fascinating, standing there in my supervisory capacity, watching the session in progress. Fergus, having got the lights fixed, his plate camera set up, and his hearing aid adjusted, got the shooting under way. And it was interesting to observe that every time he turned away to do something connected with his equipment our

cover subject would give a little shrug which would cause her
blouse to become more off-the-shoulder. As the picture taking progressed, each time that Fergus returned to look into
his camera again after getting a new plate or some such thing,
it was obvious from his reaction that things looked mighty
different in his viewfinder. By that time her blouse had become so décolleté that there was only a fraction of an inch to
go before the moment of truth, he gave me a plaintive look,
as if to say, "This *is* a family magazine, isn't it?"

The picture was a success and it made an excellent cover.
She was the type you just couldn't take a bad picture of. She
would have looked sexy in a parka. Flash Harry, our regular
glamour man, was so intrigued by her looks that he had her
in to do some pictures himself. They were spectacular. But of
course not for us. He gave her some blowups and we learned
later she sent these off to Hollywood. We didn't learn it from
her. In fact we didn't hear from her again, for she was yet
another case of someone going places who ignored the Win-
chell advice to "be nice to the people you meet on the way
up because they're the people you meet on the way down."

A couple of years passed and we had virtually forgotten
about her when somebody in a bit part in a film I saw looked
familiar and sure enough it was our girl. And in due course
stardom, with all the trappings of publicity about marriages,
divorces, custody of the children, etc.

That would have been the end of this little story, had it
not been for the fact that just the other day I happened to
notice that she cropped up in a further example of what has
now become a newspaper cliché. Whenever a features editor
is short of ideas he can always trot out that one which calls
for doing a symposium on various female stars of stage and
screen and asking them why, if they do, they consent to full
frontal nudity and, if they don't, would they if a producer
pressed them to? "If it's an integral part of the plot, essential
to the story, I see no objection . . ." You know the sort of
thing. Well, there was a big picture of our girl with lengthy
quote underneath, the burden of which was that she strongly

disapproved of the whole thing and in fact she had been able to convince the director of her new film, which required her to appear nude in two scenes, that the scenes could be just as effective without the nudity.

"My, how she's changed," I said to my wife.

My wife, being a woman and therefore more perspicacious about certain things, merely shrugged and said: "Obviously she's lost her figure."

Which brings us neatly back to the subject under discussion—vanity.

Although the Women's Liberationists rant about what they regard as the cattle-market aspect of beauty contests, this has no effect at all on the eagerness of the girls to parade.

Just as willingly they will respond to the advertisements asking them to send money to learn about, as a typical example: "A GORGEOUS NEW INCREASED BUSTLINE MEASUREMENT! . . . Have you ever seen an *un*alluring European farm girl? For centuries, these lovely country lasses have been developing into naturally voluptuous beauties without the aid of any artificial preparations or devices. And what these farm girls have been doing naturally, C*mp*ina can now do for you!" Who'd be without the allure of a European farm girl for the outlay of a mere $4.95 plus 55¢ for postage and handling, especially as the offer carries the additional attraction, "for rush order, please enclose 50¢ extra," ideal for the girl who, for example, realizes it's December already and she hasn't yet got her bust ready for the office Christmas party.

Of course, if you want to do an overall job, really make yourself a raving beauty from head to toe, the cost comes higher and the commercial exploiters of female vanity reach their apogee with the Charm School. You know the type of thing: "You TOO can be a Top Showroom or Photographic Model!" And poor Agnes, who has a face which is unfortunate and a figure that doesn't bear thinking about, sends in a photograph ("Even an informal snapshot will do") and gets back a letter (*and* registration form, "enclose money order or check") which informs her that she is cut out for Big Things

in the world of modeling . . . although of course it may take a
little time before she is fully ready to enter this highly competitive field. The "little time" can be as long as five years
and she can be short of several thousand dollars while being
groomed for her debut as a model. And in the courts of law
to which such exploiters are summoned, the judges have to
admit that there is nothing that can be done about it: "We
cannot legislate to protect women against their own vanity
and gullibility."

Crudity

I once remember getting a phone call from a man who said
that his firm had transferred him to the city and although we
didn't know him and his wife, we had lots of mutual friends
back home, so would we care to have dinner with them in the
apartment they had just moved into? I did not find it a very
rewarding evening. The meal was only adequate and the conversation desultory. The latter was especially so when my
wife was in the kitchen doing the "Can I help?" bit and,
alone with the man, I found our conversation had to be given
the kiss of life every few minutes with a fresh topic plucked
out of the blue.

I remarked to my wife afterward what heavy going it had
been but apparently there had been nothing desultory about
the conversation out in the kitchen. It had been virtually a
monologue in full flood on the part of the man's wife, from
which my wife learned that their sex life was completely
hopeless, her nerves were in a terrible state, her husband
couldn't get an erection and not only that, there was such-
and-such and such-and-such. . . . My wife had been furnished
with enough details about the husband's anatomy and behavior in and around the marital couch to fill a marriage coun-
selor's dossier.

I was amazed that a woman would stand there prodding
the potatoes to see if they were done and launch forth on a
clinical rundown of her sexual relations with her husband.

("He hasn't had a hard-on since Mother's Day.") It was as if, in the living room when our respective wives had gone off to the kitchen, I had said: "Well, Bill . . . now that the girls are off the scene, tell me all about your sex life with . . . what's her name again? . . . your wife."

But I should not have been amazed at this particular woman's performance. Men never go into such details about their wives, or any woman they respect. But it is a common practice with women. Bring this fact up with any single one of them and she will hasten to deny it. But when it is pointed out to her that she seems to know a lot of intimate details about why a certain couple have separated, say, or why such-and-such a girl has broken with the man who was her regular escort, she will say: "Perhaps so. But I only listen."

It is the fervent hope of every man, married or contemplating it, that the female he is linked with *does* only listen. Because the session described above, which happened to occur in the kitchen, is duplicated day after day up and down the country in the more usual setting for such exchanges—the bathroom. What man at a party has not seen a girl arrive and another girl say to her: "Jennifer! It's been *ages*! How *are* you! I'm just going to the john. Come on!" And off they go, presumably for one of them to sit in relative comfort while the other is perched on the edge of the tub, to start off on a pretty innocuous basis such as, "You know Roger and I have split up?" "You *haven't*!" and then really get down to cases.

There can be a batch of these sessions in the course of any given evening and apart from holding up production ("For heaven's sake come out of there, you two, there's a lineup out here"), it is an exclusively feminine phenomenon. I have yet to come across a single example of two normal men locking themselves in the lavatory for a chitchat. Quite to the contrary, the average man can even feel a certain sense of embarrassment if he finds himself sharing toilet facilities with another man. Rather than lingering to exchange any sort of dialogue he will make his exit at the earliest possible opportunity.

A woman will tell you that they have these locked-in-the-lavatory soirées because "that's the only place where we can get any privacy." One cannot deny that it requires real privacy before they can get down to a solid discussion of, say, the merits and demerits of a boyfriend's courting tackle.

But why do they do it? Why do they willingly, eagerly, disclose to other women the most intimate details about men with whom they are associated, while it never enters the mind of a man to reveal to another man such facts about a wife or girl friend?

The reason is basic to the whole makeup of women. They are pelvic beings. As pointed out elsewhere in this book, they are made in such a way that they are given little chance throughout their lives to take their minds off the pelvic area for any great length of time. Menstruation, vaginal deodorants, sexual satisfaction, contraception, childbirth, miscarriage, hysterectomy, cystitis . . . it's all happening down there—not just every now and then—month in, month out. Not unnaturally, it is for them a major focal point of interest and therefore one of the main continuing topics of conversation for women among themselves.

Catty-Bitchy-Vicious

The female characteristics of being catty, bitchy, and vicious are really one and the same. It is just a matter of degree.

Cattiness is pretty harmless stuff, often as not employed in that area which is such a preoccupation of women—clothes. As with:

"Just look at her—all dressed up like a well-kept grave."

"Very attractive, dear, but do you like it as well as what's being worn this year?"

"Darling! What a lovely dress. What a pity they didn't have it in your size."

English psychologist Dr. Alice Heim, in the chapter "The Mediocrity of Women" in her book *Intelligence and Personality*, wrote:

Women's alleged cattiness [Why *alleged* cattiness? It must exist, otherwise she wouldn't be going to the trouble of explaining why it exists.] . . . is largely due to their being more interested than men in the small personal pettinesses which constitute the subject of cattiness. The word connotes littleness, pettiness and the figurative use of claws, *i.e.*, spiteful utterances. There is little doubt that women *mind* more about day-to-day personal matters. On the other hand, they have recourse to physical reprisal less rapidly than do men. They therefore use their traditional weapon—words—and "cattiness" is the result.

The "spiteful utterances" of cattiness are invariably nothing more nor less than a woman seizing the opportunity of scoring off someone she doesn't like, as with Dorothy Parker's remark to the actress who took every opportunity to parade the fact that she was pregnant, when she did have the baby: "Congratulations, dear. We knew you had it in you."

Cattiness graduates to bitchiness when it is more than just some verbal sally that doesn't do any great harm and becomes something that is really hurtful. As: "Not only has she got a moustache but she's got dandruff in it." Now, no woman is going to be happy when she learns that that has been said of her. It is fair game to make catty remarks about a woman's clothes, a hat, a hairdo—all of which can be changed. But when you get on to biting remarks about physical appearance which one is stuck with (Poor Jessie, she's got air-cooled teeth), that's starting to get *bitchy*.

In passing, incidentally, one wonders why it is that the female dog has its name taken in vain like this. Calling a glutton a *pig*, a certain type of woman a *cow*, a man a *bull*, as examples, are animal allusions that are apposite. But what has the poor female dog done to deserve the derogatory use of the word *bitch*? There is no more docile, kindly creature than a bitch. The only time such an animal displays anything approaching the behavior of what is disparagingly called a bitch is when, teeth bared, it fights for its honor, which is praiseworthy rather than something to be derided, what with that pursuit force of ghastly mutts making your afternoon stroll a misery.

Albeit, the human bitch is out to do real harm to her victim and the way of those practices in bitchery can be misleadingly oblique and circuitous. As with this sort of thing:

"You know I'm your best friend, Muriel . . . I wouldn't be telling you this if I didn't like you, tremendously, so much so that I couldn't bear to see you get hurt . . . it was when you were away last week visiting your mother . . . your husband was home one day from the office, I think he had a chill or something . . . now I don't really blame *him* . . . that woman who's just moved in down the road and thinks she's such a raving beauty, she's so *pushy* . . . anyway, this day that your husband was home . . ."

What are the motives of this sort of bitch? Jealous of the glamour puss who got into bed with her friend's husband, which is something *she* would like to have done? Has her friend slighted her in some way and she wishes to get back at her? The motivation of the bitch is often hard to fathom but the damage that can be done by such unsolicited tip-offs in the name of feminine friendship can be immeasurable.

I knew an English cricketer who was deemed good enough at the game to be chosen to go on tour overseas with the national side. While on tour he became involved with a female cricket enthusiast, which is not a rare occurrence. A neighbor of his wife back in England, a woman who might have been regarded as his wife's best friend, had connections in the overseas country concerned and from one of these people she got not one but several letters touching on the off-field exploits of the cricketer. After a great deal of soul-searching by the woman who was just bursting to pass on this tittle-tattle she had received (it always calls for a great deal of soul-searching before coming to the decision to be a thorough bitch), she decided she must tell the wife, for her own good. This she duly did, which was to wreck that marriage.

The divorced cricketer was hooked by the camp follower and became unutterably miserable because he really loved his wife and the overseas escapade, even as an escapade, had to his mind been wearing a bit thin toward the end of the tour. The woman who got him wound up miserable, too, because she soon realized that he didn't really love her, his heart was still with his former wife, and dammit she had passed up the chance of marrying a well-to-do local scion by setting out to ensnare the dashing English cricketer. And the cricketer's ex-wife, who married again, was miserable, too, because she was still very much in love with him, and her new husband in turn was miserable because he realized he did not have her full affection, carrying that torch as she was.

Which wasn't bad going for the bitch who had gone to the wife as her best friend to impart some information for her own good—four people made lastingly unhappy.

Why men don't do that sort of thing we'll come to in a moment, after we have touched on this aspect of women at its worst level—the viciousness that women indulge in, things they do which make one shake one's head incredulously and say, "How on earth could she do a thing like that?"

Everyone has encountered numerous examples of this. I will relate just one here. It was described by the playwright John Osborne in an article he wrote for one of the Sunday papers. The piece was on his father and to me, it is one of the best things he has ever done. It was written with the warmth and humanity that are not characteristic of his plays and made one feel that if he had allowed that side of his talent full rein he would now be a great writer instead of merely a talked about one.

John Osborne's father was a commercial artist. From the time Osborne senior was a youngster his big interest was drawing and painting and his mother strongly disapproved of his intention to take up anything as flighty, to her way of thinking, as art for a career rather than something solid like banking or commerce. But when he was sixteen he won a

drawing competition in a newspaper for which the prize was
a week's holiday in South Africa. Grudgingly she allowed him
to accept the prize and he set off by ship to Cape Town. He
had a weak chest (he was to die of TB in his thirties) and
when the ship was in the Bay of Biscay he became so ill that
he had to be put ashore at Lisbon. The six weeks he spent in
hospital there ran up a bill of £200 and the hospital authorities would not release him until the money had been paid in
cash. Not being well-off (Osborne wrote that his grandparents
spent their time scrounging off the rest of the family), they
were hard put to it to raise the money. Eventually they managed to scrape it together and the boy came home. "My
grandmother never let him hear the last of that £200," wrote
Osborne.

It conjures up a frightening picture of a woman, whose son
is dying of TB, hounding him about his perfidy, nagging him,
dinning it into him, while any men present can only stand by,
knowing it is useless to try to halt the tongue-lashing. There
is nothing one can do about the vicious woman with the bit
in her teeth.

Why is it that this catty-bitchy-vicious cycle, which is
found in varying degrees in every woman, is not also a male
characteristic?

I would only partially accept the explanation put forward
by Dr. Alice Heim and others that women, lacking men's
physical strength, do with their tongues what men do with
their fists.

An equally important factor, I think, is that they have the
time to do it. It is an outgrowth of the pettiness, the preoccupation with the trivial, which besets the bulk of women
through their having to put their minds to *something* to fill in
their time. As we shall see with hoarding a mad and other
women's characteristics that are basically a product of their
having time on their hands, if you're going to be a real bitch
you have to devote considerable thought to it—rankling over
the slight *she* has done to you, thinking up ways you can get
back at her, etc.

Men might on occasion be prompted to behave in a way that would be the masculine equivalent of being bitchy but invariably they get caught up in something more rewarding with which to occupy their minds and never get around to it.

It is like that situation which often crops up in men's lives. A man hates a superior at his office or wherever he works. He vows that if he ever gets a better job elsewhere he will take great delight in striding into that bastard's office and telling him where he gets off, or better still, do something that will really fix him. But when the time comes, invariably a man will say to himself, "Why bother?" and get on with immersing himself in his new job.

6   KEEP YOUNG AND BEAUTIFUL

Eddie Cantor sang it some thirty years ago. "Keep young and beautiful, if you want to be loved." And ever since, any girl who heard him sing it has been trying desperately to cling to his advice. Just as women have throughout the ages, even if without the help of today's highly developed cosmetic and allied industries.

On the following pages is a chart of the False Front, all the artificial aids with which women concern themselves, from top to toe, in the name of Beauty Care. And for comparison, the sparse male equivalents.

Any given woman might say, "Nonsense! I don't use all those things." But an interesting little test would be for her to tick off those which she does, and be honest in not overlooking any jars, tubes, or bottles of products with which she has dallied and which are still among her collection, even if now not a regular part of her makeup. I think it would be safe to say that any woman who makes this test and claims to be involved with less than three-quarters of those things on the list is either lying or in the eyes of her female associates looks an awful sight.

THE FALSE FRONT

Women	*Men*
Hair tinting, dyeing and bleaching	Hairpieces
Wigs and hairpieces	Hair oil
Hairpins, bobby pins, etc.	(virtually
Curlers and rollers	obsolete now)
Hairsprays	
Hair conditioning creams	

Eyebrow plucking, eyebrow pencils
Eye shadow
False eyelashes, implants
Mascara, eyeliners

Ear-piercing

Facial creams and lotions	Aftershave lotion
Conditioners, moisturizers, astringents	
Pancake makeup	
Lipstick, lip gloss	
Rouge, blusher	
Face powder	
Facial depilatories	
Blemish sticks	
Mudpacks	
Chinstraps	

Perfume
Toilet water

Underarm deodorants
Underarm depilatories

Hand lotions
Nail polish
Cuticle remover
Nail conditioners
False fingernails

Falsies
Breast developers
Hormone creams
Cleavage makeup

Girdles, corselets, etc.	Girdles and supports
Reducing rollers	(rare, except
Reducing pills	among TV stars,
	symphony con-
	ductors)

Vaginal deodorants

Leg-hair removers
Toenail polish

Looking over on the men's side of the ledger it is really staggering to note the minute number of artificial aids men call upon in contrast to women. An immediate feminine reaction might be: "But wait a minute! What about all those ads for men's cosmetics?" I have not included in the men's list those modern aids to male beauty which I agree are on the market. How many men use them? I have been afforded a good yardstick on this by the fact that my wife, as a women's magazine editor, is showered with free samples of cosmetics —men's as well as women's. Naturally she gets nowhere when she tries to unload the stuff on me. But what is revealing is this: Even our grown-up sons shake their heads and say, "Thank you very much all the same." Our daughter can't find a boyfriend who is thrilled to take the stuff over. Even that pioneer of men's cosmetics—aftershave lotion—has been found to be a slow mover.

I think the ultimate in the attempt to get men interested in cosmetics is to be seen in the advertisements now being run by the manufacturers of one of the leading vaginal deodorants. They have brought out a "personal deodorant" for men. In the advertisements women are urged to put their men on to a good thing, which "works for him the way yours works for you" at "the most sensitive area of his body—the genital area." It seems that this "private deodorant spray" (a lovely choice of words) will keep him "fresh, cool, and confident all day."

All one can say to *that* is: Really, girls, you mustn't try to foist your problems on to us men.

There is hardly a square inch of a woman's body that she doesn't do something about, and before going on to treat in detail with the various aspects about the chart . . .

I think one of the most interesting things it indicates is all the attention given to the eyes. It stands to reason that the hair, for example, calls for a lot of work, since there is so much of it. But the eyes, a relatively small part of the anatomy, may justifiably be said to be a feminine preoccupation. And for what? Is there a man among us who doesn't wish to hell they would leave them alone?

Some readers may raise their eyebrows at the inclusion of Cleavage Makeup. But, so help me, it's true. Females *can* buy a busty equivalent of eye shadow, for applying to the cleavage and thus, they hope, kidding the troops that their breasts must be wonderfully big because of the deep shadow they cast down in the valley. I am not lying.

Not included on the chart is another product, which does not exist. Not yet, anyway. But what with all this frontal nudity and one thing and another, I think it is only a matter of time before some manufacturer is smart enough to put on the market a tinting concoction that will come to the help of those women who fret terribly about the fact that their pubic hairs are starting to turn gray. It is about the only thing that the cosmeticians haven't yet thought of.

Beauty Is Only Skin Dope

Pick up any women's magazine or turn to the women's pages
of any newspaper and you'll see it there—the Beauty Column.
At random I've chosen a column written by a good lady who
calls herself Mary Collins. Heading for this week's offering is
"How to Face Up to Your Complexion" (brilliant!) and the
opening paragraph reads:

The woman with a clear, glowing complexion is a beautiful
woman. No matter how irregular her features, her teeth or
her figure it's her skin that people notice first and this is what
they will remember.

How right you are, Mary. Time and again one sees a
knock-kneed, flat-chested, hook-nosed, buck-toothed lass go
walking by and the lads on the street corner let out with the
wolf whistles and say to one another: "Wow! What a terrific
complexion!"

It really is guff, isn't it, this stuff these women write and
which presumably Mary's millions of readers lap up. Paragraph 2 runs:

It's hard work keeping the complexion in good condition.
Makeup, central heating, dirt and grime in the air—all these
things can cause problems that must be dealt with each day if
you want to present a pretty face to the world.

The significant thing about that is that it is *makeup* that
heads the list of things that wreak havoc on the feminine
face. This having been established, what does Mary then do?
Without batting an eyelash she then proceeds to list by brand
name and go into detail about nine products with which
women can do further damage to their faces.

How can it be expected of skin to stand up to day after
day of conditioning, moisturizing, refining with astringent lotion, "normalizing," and all the other daubing and scraping
away that it is subjected to?

The sad day comes for a man when he may perhaps get up
early one day and happen to look at the face of his sleeping

wife in an unguarded moment and realize that the facade has collapsed. All the things she has been doing to her face to keep young and beautiful are the very things which have caused her no longer to look young and beautiful.

Curlers

Throughout the evolution of curlers, from the primitive rolling of strands of hair around bits of newspaper, through the clamping of locks in pieces of cloth-covered, malleable metal to the tubular curlers with attached elastic band and finally to the modern roller, throughout the entire history of this aid to feminine beauty the sight of a woman in curlers is probably the thing a man most dislikes about any aspect of herself she presents to him.

The intelligent woman, knowing how abhorrent it is to men, does it as furtively as possible. But the horrifying development we are now confronted with is that many women are to be seen out and about in broad daylight with their rollers on. She gets out of her car at the supermarket looking as impeccable as her shiny new auto, her formclinging pants suit fresh from the cleaners, her blouse immaculately pressed—and she's wearing rollers!

It is a weird sort of feminine logic whereby a woman can convince herself that it is all right for her to thus make herself look hideous during the day in order to have a crowning glory of curls for a few hours in the evening, at a party or whatever the great occasion is. If a husband dare draw attention to this, she will say: "You want me to look nice, don't you!" To which the answer of course is: "Yes—all the time you're on view to the public." It is a certainty that she never showed herself to *him* in curlers in the days when their courtship was in full flood.

Not only is the effect on men dire. Think of the poor kids. Young daughter Ann, with the burst of emotion not uncommon in young girls, suddenly says, "Oh, Mommy, I love you," and goes over to fling her arms around the object of her affection. And what does she get? A faceful of hard plastic rollers. Apart from the physical injury the poor kid is likely to sustain, think of the psychological effect. According to the psychiatrists the Mother Image is warm, soft, and cuddlesome. The plastic-metal-spiky connotation of rollers cuts right across this. It would seem obvious that the young child would be repelled by the sight and feel of the things. But the psychiatrists know better than that. They know that there is also that driving force within young Ann to emulate the Mother Figure. So instead of revulsion, it is: "Gee, Mom, I'm six already and you haven't yet got me rollers."

We men can only look on and sadly shake our roller-free heads, for it would seem that there is now a feeling in many female minds that the curler, in its modern roller form, has reached a stage of its development which has taken it beyond being merely utilitarian. It is now ornamentation. Draped becomingly in a headscarf, rollers can now be worn as an adornment.

In time we men will doubtless learn to go along with this. After all, haven't the Ubangi tribesmen become conditioned to thinking that the lip discs of their womenfolk look great?

The Bleached Blonde

It is interesting how a person can say one sentence, perhaps just a casual remark, which is so evocative—illuminating, say, or frightening or nostalgic—that it sticks in one's mind. When I was interviewing a woman in connection with a book I was writing she said something, purely in passing, which I have always remembered. She was speaking of a nervous breakdown she had and she said: "There I was, feeling utterly miserable, with five weeks of black root . . ."

Five weeks of black root . . . how vividly that one simple phrase epitomized the fact that women are slaves to the artificial front they present to the world.

Women of course will recognize at once what "five weeks of black root" means, but for the sake of men lucky enough not to be aware of such things it should be explained that "black root" is how women refer to hair growing through in its natural color at the roots when a bleached blonde doesn't keep up her bleaching assiduously.

When this woman used the phrase it presented to my mind's eye the awful scene of women in prisons, hospitals, mental homes, and in other circumstances in which they can't keep up their bleach religiously. What an awful, depressing sight it must be—whole batches of women with a straight line drawn across the strands of their hair, one part black and the other blonde, looking like nothing God ever created. Completely unnatural because nothing in nature, be it noted, is ever in a straight line.

Why women want to be blonde in the first place heaven alone knows. If it is to make themselves more attractive to men they are acting on a false premise. Men like blondes, certainly. The natural, Scandinavian type. But what the girls who bleach overlook is that there are two main things about hair—color and, perhaps even more important than color, texture. When you go blonde you say goodbye to texture. If a girl is out to please a man she should remember that her hair is not merely to look at. Also it is to touch. But when a man runs his fingers through a bleached blonde's hair he always feels there is the risk of getting splinters in his fingers. Strawlike, brittle, and unyielding.

Women are always getting themselves involved in vicious circles when it comes to keeping up their false front. Having bleached and ruined the natural texture of their hair they find themselves stuck with that awful flaxen thatch which they know, without the TV commercials dinning it into them, is "unmanageable." So—having put on lotions that ruin the texture of their hair, they then put on another set of lotions to try to restore the texture. It is the sort of nonsense encountered in automobile accessories shops where you can buy special bumpers to fit on to your bumpers to stop the bumpers from getting bumped.

An added reason why the attractiveness of the Scandinavian type blonde is unattainable by artificial means is that they are the golden girls, *i.e.*, they have "overall" complexions, a creamy skin coloring that is uniform, rather than the pink-and-white variety. The overall complexion tans beautifully and there are few girls who look as striking as the genuine blonde with a good tan—either outdoors or, say, in a simple white dress indoors. Makeup becomes entirely unnecessary and they achieve that perfection of beauty—the type that can stand under a shower and none of the beauty washes off. Those debating whether they should go blonde should realize that if you haven't got that naturally, you just can't get it artificially. All you wind up with as the years go by is the automatic association in people's minds with the worst aspects of the artificial blonde—the tart, the hash-house waitress, and the showbiz has-been.

Self-Torture

There is no limit to the things women will do to themselves and have done to them in their dedicated determination to look young and beautiful.

To ensure that their feet look shapely they squash them into shoes that may have beautiful lines but which bear no relation to the true shape of the foot. Painful as this may be it is as nothing compared to the agony of what results, which not without reason has given rise to the comment that hell has no fury like a woman's corn. Her feet having been held contorted as in a vise inside her "fashionable" shoes, they eventually become permanently misshapen and you may be sure that the most unattractive part of any woman—even though she may be an acknowledged beauty—are her ill-treated feet.

The torture they subjected themselves to in order to get the wasp waist that was the vogue of former years is something they don't have to go through now. But even if elasti-

barrels of dried fruits, everything on delightful unhygienic display. What does a supermarket smell of? Nothing. Unless you happen to be there when somebody drops a bottle of nice spicy chutney or some such thing on the concrete floor.

The speed with which an odor can conjure up pictures . . . I remember one time at a hotel when I was passing through the lobby I suddenly started thinking about Casablanca. I had no great reason to do this, since I had only been there once many years before and then only briefly between planes, just long enough to realize that it is about as glamorous and exotic as Oshkosh, Wisconsin. I happened to go through that hotel lobby again a little later and at precisely the same spot Casablanca flashed into my mind again.

This puzzled me and after I had given it some thought I went up to a couple who were sitting there. He was a dull, dumpy looking fellow and she was attractive, so I figured it was best to talk to him rather than her, in case he might read anything into it.

"I hope you don't mind my asking this," I said to him, "but I wonder if you could tell me what perfume your wife is using."

"Chanel No. 5, I should think," he said. "It's her favorite, she tells me."

He was unfriendly, suspicious, so I withdrew. It was a while after that when I was sitting alone in the lobby that she was walking by me on some errand and she paused.

"As a matter of fact," she said, "it's a scent from Casablanca that a friend gave me."

She smiled and then went on her way.

Any taxi driver will tell you that he likes having a woman with good perfume use his cab—it makes the male customers who follow happy. A cabby philosopher of my acquaintance, who says that it is essential for women to use perfume "since a woman without perfume is like a vase without flowers," told me: "Men feel they're getting a bonus, something for free included in the cost of the ride. I often take a look around, and there's our friend taking a nice deep breath with a faraway look in his eyes."

With this potent weapon at their disposal, girls should make the most of it. At the risk of sounding like "Hints on How to Get Your Man" . . .

When you are entertaining that young man who has shown interest in you and you are hopeful that the interest will ripen and flourish, here is a novel way to use perfume. You have invited him to your flat and all is ready—a dreamy LP already under way on the record player, soft lights, the wine —that's when you add the final touch! Get your bottle of perfume and put a little dab on each light bulb. What is achieved is that *your* perfume pervades the whole room. Your fragrance is everywhere. Even when you are reclining on the couch and he goes over to change the records—you are *there*, because the light by the record player is wafting out *Nuit d'Amour*, the scent he subconsciously always associates with you. It is all terribly subtle. The poor fellow doesn't know what's getting to him.

But a word of warning. Don't put too much scent on each bulb. If you do, when the bulbs really heat up the smell of perfume can become overpowering. And also, if you really douse the light with perfume there is the danger of it cracking and there is nothing more disconcerting than an electric bulb blowing up just when the magic moment has arrived.

The great thing about perfuming electric bulbs is that it has a two-way function. It can be done to get that promising male guest into the right mood, or it can be used as a dissuader. A married woman I know has been using it for years and her husband hasn't yet tumbled to it. He is something of an explorer when attractive women are around and it is her way of keeping him in check. When they are giving a party she always puts a little of her perfume on the bulbs. As the party progresses he starts to show interest in, say, that glamorous young lady in the low-cut gown sitting under the floor lamp over in the corner. But he is seen to shake his head as though something is not quite right. Everything is set to make a play for this girl in the secluded corner—but he keeps thinking of his wife. Of course he does. Her perfume is wafting to him with every intake of breath. Without his knowing why, a whole damper is put on his intentions.

Incidentally, she always, as a form of extra insurance, puts some of her perfume on the bedside light in the spare bedroom.

Bosom Interest

As we entered the 1970's an effort was being made to release the breasts from their traditional harness. Women's (Burn the Bras) Lib may claim some of the credit for this, but rightfully the credit should go to the Permissive Society. Sad to say, however, the granting of liberty to the breasts touches only a minute proportion of women.

The trend setters, the swinging chicks will let it be seen that they have nothing on under their T-shirts but the vast majority of females are still faithfully wedded to their bras.

There are two basic reasons for this.

One is that the bust is the epitome of the False Front. The woman who can't be bothered with false eyelashes, say, or false fingernails will most certainly feel that it is of paramount importance that she falsify her bust—if old and blowzy, for instance, she will wear a bra to give the amorphous mass some sort of shape and if young, to make her bust more effective as what Desmond Morris calls "a sexual signaling device." With a high proportion of women, if the bra were taken away the truth would come out. Many girls would reveal that they literally have nothing to hide. At the other end of the scale a girl would let it be seen that her breasts are so unattractively bulgy that her bra is in truth a double-topper wobble-stopper. Others would be seen to be saggy. A dozen and one considerations which prevent women as a whole from presenting the no-bra look.

And the other basic reason—the nipples. This is something which women are very self-conscious about. Although in 1970 it was felt that the Permissive Society had reached a stage whereby store dummies in the display windows of women's dress shops could be equipped with nipples, instead of those odd looking nippleless dummies one used to see naked when a store window was being changed, this breakthrough has actually had no great effect on the female's fundamental attitude toward her nipples. A woman who has long been in the brassiere business told me: "The two parts of a woman which she is most embarrassed about are her nipples and the Gap, that bit of thigh above her stocking tops." As dealt with elsewhere in this book, women have to a degree overcome their concern about the Gap with that terrible pantyhose. But the nipples she has always managed to keep anonymous within her bra. In fact rarely, throughout the entire history of women's clothing, have they ever in actuality or even in outline shown to the world their, to them, offending protruders. So the attitude of the bulk of women today is: Why should we start now, by adopting the no-bra look?

Why on earth they have this thing about their nipples, don't ask me. No woman I talked to during my researches could give me a logical explanation. One women's liberationist said: "They remind a woman of having babies and rearing them and that's something she doesn't want to be reminded of." Which seemed a typically unfeminine attitude from such as they. More logical perhaps is that the nipples are the only clearly visible erectile part of their anatomy and they would rather keep their personal reactions to themselves.

The brassiere then, for the reasons stated above, is here to stay, to continue to be, as far as men are concerned, among the least attractive aspect of women in clothes.

The brassiere's history lies entirely within this century and there is an interesting reason why it did not need to exist before the 1910's, and then just had to be invented.

The bust used to be supported by the corset, in its secondary role. The primary job of the corset was of course to provide a slim waist. This was achieved by tightly lacing the midriff inside the garment, with its stays of long, narrow lengths of bone or steel. These stiffeners had to be long, long enough to come up above the rib cage, for the simple reason that if they didn't, women would be stabbing themselves in the stomach every time they leaned forward. Therefore it was not really by design but just by coincidence that the top of the corset happened to be in a position to support the bust. And this it did for centuries.

But then, early this century, some bright spark came up with a process for extruding rubber in such a way that it could be woven with thread, from which material could be made that had "two-way stretch." Thus was born "elasticized material," which is now "stretch fabric" in its modern development. The exciting new two-way stretch material was seized upon by the corset manufacturers as something which would do the job of holding madam's waist in, without the necessity of those frightful bones or steels.

Originally, however, the manufacturers kept to the concept that it must be a long, hip-to-bosom garment like the one it was replacing and some time was to elapse before it dawned on them that it could perform its waist-slimming function as a more abbreviated piece of attire. What was happening, of course, was that the girdle was getting itself born, but what we are concerned with here is what was going on up top. Obviously when the corset shrank in size the breasts were left stranded up there all on their own. An entirely new garment, for the bust alone, had to come into being. The brassiere.

The ironic thing was that it had only just started on its career of supporting and therefore heightening the bust both literally and as a sexual signaling device, when it was called upon to do just the opposite. The flat-chested look of the 1920's came into vogue and the brassiere was pressed into service as a constricting harness to get rid of the bosom contours. At that time the bust wasn't needed as an area of enticement. With the skirts as short as they were, the legs were very capably looking after all the sexual signaling. Fashions change. In the 1930's the skirts went down and bosom interest was back. And the women of the period were astute in the way they handled it, so much so that the 1930's are remembered by those who lived through them as a time when women were at their most attractively feminine. Without perhaps fully realizing what they were doing, they took cognizance of the fact that the vertical lines are the beautiful ones (church spires, poplar trees, etc.) and the horizontal ones are not, as exemplified by the bobbed hair and sawed-off skirts of the females of the 1920's.

The women of the 1930's wore their hair long, their dresses long. A typical evening gown would have narrow shoulder straps and a deep V-neck directing the eye down to that major focal point of male interest, the bosom. The bras of the time contrived to improve the appearance of the breasts but to leave them looking accurate and clearly pliant, as God had made them—not the contorted things inflicted upon us by Lana Turner and the bra manufacturers, as we will see when we come to the 1940's. Very craftily, the material of those evening gowns was cut on the bias, a term that I as a man was not familiar with until it was explained to me. Suffice to say, it is the way material is cut for nightgowns, so the association in the male mind was automatic. The result of all this, as can be seen among the young ladies who inhabited those old Fred Astaire and Ginger Rogers films shown on TV, was the very feminine Willowy Look. In contrast to bumping up against the unyielding False Front of today, dancing with a girl in those days was an Event.

Never was a strapless evening gown worn, never that jarring horizontal line of the top of the dress cutting across the bosom, and this wise concentration on the vertical lines the women of the 1930's carried over into the bathing suit. The bikini, thankfully, was unheard of and it is interesting that in modern times women are going back to the one-piece swimsuit of the 1930's, realizing that if looking alluringly feminine be your aim, much more can be achieved with it than with the bikini.

In the bathing suit of the 1930's the uncupped breasts hung normally, so that it was not necessary for a man to say to himself, as now, that with luck he'll find out what they are like when she is not in her cups. And from behind, the Suntan Back which Mr. Jantzen evolved and which was in fact nothing from the nape of the neck to the base of the spine let the whole world see the gracious line of a woman's naked back, unmarred by the unattractive back strapping of the bikini.

But to return to the front, in which we are mainly interested in this section, in the 1940's things took a turn for the worse. And it is probably Lana Turner, the original Sweater Girl of the 1940's, who may be regarded as the chief culprit in furthering the idea that women should contort their breasts into shapes which Mother Nature in her wisdom never envisaged. The outcome of Lana Turner constantly parading her particular type of false front on the screen and in pinups was that the girls of the world took to presenting us with sweater-encased twin cones which bore no recognizable relationship to breasts as God made them. One wondered to whom the girls thought these jutting cones appealed. They certainly did not appeal to men. Men noticed them, granted. But they did not look at them to admire but to try to visualize what they would look like when released from their harness, very much the way one would look at a building of good basic design ruined by the addition of unnecessary architectural rhubarb. Breasts are pendant, pliant spheres, not rock-hard, conic protuberances.

This phenomenon of the late 1940's, from which even today we are far from free, was of course linked with the great bosom interest which burgeoned in the immediate postwar era and in this regard one must be wary of the pronouncements of psychiatrists. They can talk the most utter rubbish. An example of this is their explanation of why, after

World War II, women placed such an accent on the bosom. Along with Lana Turner we had Jane Russell at the forefront of this. It seemed that no sooner had hostilities ceased than the copious Russell bosom, photographed from every conceivable angle, became one of the main preoccupations of the nations. With this incentive, large upperworks became *the* thing. Those women who had them were in their heyday; those who didn't have them rallied to falsie manufacturers such as the firm which advertised, "What God has forgotten we stuff with cotton." Clothes were designed to draw every bit of attention to them, from cleavage to platform bras which their wearers fondly imagined projected their bosoms up and out but in truth merely resulted in jelly on a shelf.

Why all this accent on the bosom? The psychiatrists were called in and came up with this explanation: "The masculinity of war made women want to be ultra-feminine when it was all over, to present to the men back from the wars femininity in its broadest aspect." This made sense ... until you gave it some thought for a moment or two and the question popped into your mind: "If that was so, why was it that after the *first* World War women did exactly the opposite, flattening their bosoms and bobbing their hair and looking as *masculine* as possible?" But one could probably get a psychiatrist to talk his way out of that one with the same facility as that of opinion pollsters explaining that although they forecast an election incorrectly, they really got it right.

In the 1950's disaster overtook the brassiere in the form of the molded bra—that type of garment in which each breast is fitted into a precast cup of stiffened material which is supposed to conform to the ideal of alluring roundness. The molded bra has virtually rendered the falsie obsolete, since it doesn't really matter what you stick into those cups. If the breasts are modest in size they can just sit in there with what Robert Service in another context called "space to leap and play," while outwardly the molded cups present their picture of a "perfect" bust, as unyielding as a metal breastplate.

Not content just with fitting their bosoms into preshaped

containers when in sweater, blouse, or dress, they went along with the idea of doing the same thing in swimwear, and the molded bra built into bathing suits is one of the least happy things which women, in pursuance of the False Front, have ever resorted to. It really does look terrible, doesn't it, when you see an otherwise attractive girl cavorting on the beach and the natural movements of her bust become quite unrelated to her stiffly bra-topped swimsuit until she has her breasts here, there, and everywhere and she has to take time out to get them fitted back into that awful built-in bra.

The brassiere reached the stage of development whereby there was the distorted attitude that the bust was made for bras, not bras for the bust; it is something that has persisted through to today. As mentioned at the start, an attempt has been made to release it from its harness. Also there is the bra for the "softer look," a flimsy sort of nothing-bra which is an effort to give women the more natural, more pleasing look of the 1930's. But such attempts to break from the trussed-up, phony look have unfortunately not got wide acceptance. Study females out and about and you will see that the majority of them are still hooked on, or rather hooked into, the artificial preshaped brassiere which uniformly deprives their bosoms of all character.

Rock Bottom

Of all the garments in which women encase themselves, the worst in the eyes of men is undoubtedly the girdle. It is a gross offense against aesthetics.

All right, the girdle has a reason for being, a three-fold reason, but that does not convince men that that justifies its existence.

The girdle has three functions: (a) to flatten the stomach, (b) to restrain the posterior, and (c) to keep the stockings up. We can forget about the last named, since it is only seconded to that job because it happens to be there.

As to (a), the flattening of the stomach, it does that job efficiently only on a female who doesn't really need to wear one. Convincing women who have gone to fat that such things as the new multiple-elasticated Flatto girdle will make the stomach look as flat as that of an undernourished virgin is one of the greatest con tricks that has ever been pulled. You cannot make solid flesh disappear. You can only displace it. Bulging women's stomachs contorted within girdles take on an odd, unnatural look. Something akin to the pregnancy look but quite distinguishable from it. After all, a pregnant woman is at the height of her womanliness and has no cause to feel embarrassed about her appearance. But matronly women executives, platform speakers at the Women's Institute, political gatherings, etc., aging actresses and others who truss up their stomachs in the girdle and its big sister, the foundation garment, carry before them something that gets nowhere near their goal of flatness but is merely a weirdly shaped pot that bears no relation to anything in the anatomy books.

Squashing their spare tire into a different shape inside a girdle may be pardoned on the score that the stomach has never been a great focal point of aesthetic or sexual interest. But what they use the girdle for, (b), as regards their bottoms is absolutely unforgivable.

A woman's bottom in a girdle loses all its character. It can at least be said in defense of the brassiere that it does leave the breasts with their individuality, does highlight the fact that the bust is what Desmond Morris in *The Naked Ape* terms a "sexual signaling device." But what right have women to say that God made their bottoms wrongly that instead of pliant twin buttocks, what should be presented to the world, with the aid of a girdle, is one great convex spread as hard as a rock and as unyielding to the touch as an over-inflated beach ball?

Personally, I am not a callipygalist (kal-i-PIDGE-al-ist, from the Greek, meaning an admirer of beautiful posteriors). I can take bottoms, or leave them alone. But I must join with the callipygalist (or put more bluntly, a Bottom Man) in registering a protest against the desecration by women of what to many men is a thing of beauty.

The admiration of a shapely pair of buttocks goes back thousands of years, as evidenced by that piece of ancient Greek sculpture known as "the Callipygalous Venus," of which the posterior is the dominant aspect. In more recent times the vogue of the bustle last century confirmed the interest that is there. Even more recently Marilyn Monroe and other exponents of the Wiggle have drawn attention to that zone. A gentleman who worked for a firm of falsie manufacturers even managed to convince his employers that there could be a lucrative untapped market in buttock falsies. They were put on sale, but never caught on. Of course they didn't. The woman of today is far too firmly wedded to her girdle. Elizabeth Taylor's attempt to strike a blow for freedom from the girdle for those broad in the beam with her "what the hell, why not cooperate with the inevitable" attitude gathered few followers around her.

The really shocking thing about it all is that, as is the case with hair rollers, Mom is inflicting the girdle upon her female offspring. Her lithe, svelte daughter who has no need of it whatsoever is cocooned into one and apart from its being a crime against aesthetics, she is thus condemning the poor child to premature atrophy of muscles not allowed to undertake the functions that they are there for.

Perfection

Before leaving this subject of "Keep Young and Beautiful" it should be pointed out that women would be justified in saying that it is men who contribute in no small measure to their necessity to put up a false front. Man cannot stand imperfections in women.

I remember seeing a very attractive girl in the dining car of a train. So attractive, in fact, that I inwardly cursed the waiter for showing me to another table and not to the vacant place opposite her. I envied the man who did take the seat at her table, for in no time an acquaintance was struck up. She revealed herself as being alert, with a wonderful smile and a sort of charm she exuded, which got to me even at the distance I was away, so I could only guess how enchanted her tablemate was at close quarters. Their meal went on for some time, including appropriate wines and liqueurs suggested by her newly found friend. Not to put too fine a point on it, I was green with envy, for obviously she was a girl of good background and not the pick-up type. So fascinated was I by her that I, too, lingered over my meal, having a second after-lunch coffee. And still they sat there, chatting away cosily as though they had known each other for years. It struck me that she did not want the meal ever to end. The other tables were by now empty and the waiters were giving their customary indications of wanting us all out of there. I was about to take their hint when I learned, abruptly, why the girl had not wanted the meal to come to an end. When her new escort said, cheerily, "Shall we go?" and got up to help her from the table I saw that her left leg was enclosed in an ungainly metal clamp.

I can still see in my mind's eye the look on the face of the man. And I know that when he delivered her to her part of the train, that—as well as she knew it would be—was that.

In view of this, women feel that it is imperative for them to conceal, by every available artificial means from pancake makeup to falsies, any imperfections they have. To appear as perfect a feminine specimen as they can contrive is the way (a) to attract men, and (b) pamper the ego of any man they have attracted, by making him proud to have them on his arm.

But men don't have to bother to keep up such a false front. Women will accept them as they are. And the most dramatic way to underline the truth of this is to draw attention to this fact: if the wars were fought by women instead of men, thousands upon thousands of young women would be left on the shelf without a chance of ever getting married.

Young men come home from the war disfigured, maimed, with only one leg, only a stump for an arm, faces a horrifying pulp from burns—but this is not the end of life for them as far as marriage and having a family is concerned. Such things are no bar to a woman falling in love with a man and marrying him. But if the thousands of war wounded were women, the eligible men would turn the other way.

A woman's capacity to do this is of course tied in with what is gone into more fully elsewhere—the fact that she is born to carry two people. Here is a man who has to be looked after. Her mother instinct comes out.

Men are not motherly. But sometimes they try to be.

Some years ago in the course of my work I met an actress of quite astounding beauty. She had had a riding accident which left her paralyzed from the waist down. But when she learned that she would have to spend the rest of her life in a wheelchair it did not prevent her from pursuing her acting career as actively as before, in radio. A young man who had just finished his service as an Air Force pilot married her and it was touching to see the care and attention he would lavish upon her when he would bring her to the studio, see that she got coffee and something to eat during the breaks and then, after the broadcast, carry her in his arms out to the car to place her in the front seat beside him.

The years go by. One day recently I was enjoying the view at a holiday resort when a man approached me. He called me by name and said, "I bet you don't remember *me*." The face, which was lined and appeared prematurely old, was familiar and I tried to pinpoint it as a younger face. Then after he had given me a couple of hints I realized that it was the pilot who had married the girl in the wheelchair.

"Good to see you again," I said. "How is . . . ?" Usually not good at remembering names, for once I remembered this one. "How's Sylvia?"

Abruptly he looked ashamed, as if found out. "I'm not married to her now. You must meet Margaret. She'll be along in a minute, as soon as she's put the youngsters to bed."

7 THE SEXUAL PREDICAMENT

The sexual pattern of women is so different from and so much more complex than that of men that not only are men so often at a loss to fathom it, women themselves can be very much at sea as to what makes them tick sexually. Here and in following chapters we deal with this aspect of the feminine syndrome, starting with one of the fundamental differences in male and female attitudes.

Visual Stimulation

Men are constantly stimulated *visually*. Shapely legs, well-formed breasts, neatly turned buttocks, even if fully clothed, will sexually excite him *on sight*. Women do not react in the same way. A woman will make approving note of a handsome face, good hands, a well-shaped back (women are just crazy about men's backs), but the progression is not for her to be sexually stimulated by what she sees. The next step is to talk to him. A woman must talk to a man and through conversation assess his background, his approach to life, his general suitability, before she can decide whether or not he is really attractive to her.

Behind this fundamental difference lies the fact that put in simple terms, a man is looking for a girl he can sleep with that night, while a girl is looking for a life partner.

It should be mentioned that we are of course dealing here with the generality of women, not with the type of female of whom it can be said that the story of her life is an open bed.

That this basic difference between men and women exists is not arrived at merely from observation. It is a biological fact. Men are made constantly on the *qui vive* sexually because it is Nature's way of ensuring the propagation of the species. From the moment in his life when the young male suddenly realizes that there is something else very exciting beside baseball, construction kits, and cowboy films until his dying day a man will continue to be sexually aroused by the sight of feminine beauty in any of its manifestations. For example, if example were needed, the last act of John Barrymore on his deathbed was to make a pass at his good-looking nurse. The fact that women are not so made is for the very good reason that some sort of governor had to be placed on the machinery of procreation. As a doctor once put it to me: "If men *and* women were visually stimulated we'd be stepping over bodies having sexual intercourse all over the place."

A mother may wonder why her son is always borrowing her mail order catalog, while her daughter shows no similar interest. Being a woman, the mother doesn't stop to realize the excitements the women's underwear section of the catalog holds for her son.

If it were necessary to prove that men are constantly stimulated visually and women are not, one need only point to the proliferation of nudie magazines in the bookstores and to the striptease joints. There is no striptease for women, nothing such as "Hunk of Man" Ludovic, the Nordic Adonis, lingeringly taking his clothes off for matrons who have come into town for some shopping and want some entertainment before going back to their humdrum homelife. Women are just not interested, for you may be sure that if there were a demand for it, the gentlemen who put on striptease shows for men would be quick to cater to the womenfolk. Similarly, there is no equivalent of the nudie magazine for women, *i.e.*, endless photographs of the male form in seductive poses. (Okay, there are such mags, but we all know that they are not for the female market.) When women do feel the need of erotic stimulation it is not, as with men, achieved by perusal

of pictures of naked strangers. Women prefer to personalize
the thing by conjuring up images in their own minds of sexual excitements brought to them by men of the films and TV
or encountered in their daily lives.

Another aspect of this fact that women are not stimulated
visually is that men who indulge in indecent exposure are
fighting for a lost cause. Their whole performance is based on
the false premise that because they are excited by the sight of
an intimate part of a woman exposed, the reverse is true. It
can do nothing but land them in trouble.

A few years ago there was a court case at an English seaside resort that did not get the publicity it deserved. It was a
story of a sort that is welcomed by news editors to brighten
up the paper during the hot summer months but unfortunately it had to be spiked in those days before the present permis-
siveness that allows newspapers to be more broad-minded in
what they print.

It seems that sitting in a deck chair on the promenade by
the beach was what is called in indecent exposure circles a
"flasher." This particular flasher was helped to his performances by the fact that he was a Scotsman. He wore the kilt.
Females passing by were treated to a practiced flick of the
kilt and one girl took it upon herself to complain to the
police. The gentleman found himself in court and in the
course of giving evidence the girl said: "As I was walking past
him he lifted up his kilt and I could see his big thing." The
flasher's lawyer was no fool. In an inspired moment he put
the accused's wife on the stand. Having established that in
her more than twenty years of marriage to the accused she
had had full opportunity of observing her husband un-
clothed, at close quarters, he asked her: "With regard to your
husband's sexual organ—would you describe it as 'a big
thing'?" The involuntary burst of laughter she gave was practically all that was needed. Little legal argument was required
of the lawyer to have the case thrown out on a technicality.

So alien to women is the idea of indecently exposing themselves (except of course for strippers, nude models, and

others willing to be paid by men to do it) that it is not even
on the statute books as an offense with which they can be
charged. A man, on the other hand, can be charged with this
offense even if he is in his own home, fails to draw the
curtains and is observed naked by a woman on the street.
Since no such charge can be brought against a woman if she
does the same thing, this seemed to me to be just a little
unfair, so I checked with a police legal expert to confirm it.

"Quite true," he said.

"You mean," I said, "that a man can quite inadvertently
forget to draw the curtains and be arrested and yet a woman
can parade around naked at her open window and no charge
will be brought against her?"

"Correct. Unless of course such a big crowd collects that
she could be charged with causing a traffic obstruction."

Women can regard themselves as fortunate that they do
not suffer from the fact that this visual stimulation which
continually besets men, apart from its being a confounded
nuisance which frequently stops us from getting on with our
work, can often lead men into liaisons which are embarrassing to their friends and give rise to bitter self-condemnation.
The pattern is familiar. For example, a broker or an attorney
or other man of similar stature can get himself so worked up
about the view of the cleavage of the girl behind the bar or
the intriguing rear view of her thighs as she bends over in hot
pants that he finds himself lingering to take her home and
trying to turn a deaf ear to the smirking comments as they go
off. Parked with her in his car at the end of her depressing
street ("You can't come in, Grandpa sleeps in the front
room"), he winces every time she says "Naughty, naughty!,"
conscious that her every utterance proclaims her as being
common as dirt. "What a fool I am, why did I ever get
involved?" he chides himself as he drives away, shuddering at
the remembrance of every tawdry second of it.

There is a simple explanation for the men who suffer from
the agonies of the sexual hangover, from the Senior Partner
who intercepts the leggy stenographer behind the filing cabi-

nets at the office party to the Managing Director who returns from the disastrous illicit weekend with the bosomy cigarette girl: They will cast aside all their self-restraint and sense of decorum for something that looks good sexually.

Women do not do that sort of thing. They do not make these excursions down the social ladder through merely being sexually excited by the look of some man. Some women *do* cross the tracks for sex, but for them it is a calculated affair —the Lady Chatterley syndrome. For example, the young socialite who dallies with the garage mechanic is bored, bored with the effete young men by whom she is surrounded and wants someone for heaven's sake to pay her the compliment of giving her a real going-over.

Certain female readers of all this may tell you that it is nonsense to say that they are not sexually excited by the look of a man. My researches have indeed uncovered women who say that they are even capable of having an orgasm just from the contemplation of an attractive male stranger. But such women are rare, as rare as men who can see a girl in a low-cut dress adjust a shoe and remain unmoved.

Loneliness

One of the saddest aspects of the feminine syndrome is the damned loneliness that besets so many of them. Sitting alone in one of the chairs against the wall at the junior prom waiting for someone to come and ask you to dance . . . sharing an apartment and seeing the others go off on their Saturday night dates and eyeing the phone there stubbornly refusing to ring on your behalf . . . getting on just a little in years and overhearing snide remarks like, "I hear she's writing a book called *Live Alone And Look It*" . . . the terrible dread of going to your grave a spinster, passed up, unfulfilled, an old maid.

The male is far more fortunate in this regard. He has a much better deal. He doesn't need to wait for the phone to ring, he can go out on his own. If the years go by and he's unmarried, there is no stigma attached. In fact he can be a subject of envy. He is a gay blade playing the field. "You lucky devil, you've got your freedom."

But we know that women don't have a monopoly on loneliness. The aging gay blade with his freedom can get mighty sick and tired of coming home to his empty bachelor apartment. The young man who doesn't need to wait for the phone to ring can return many a time from being out and about and bemoan the fact that nothing materialized.

And don't think that husbands, surrounded by family and friends, at home and at work, are not beset by loneliness, for the greatest cause for them of that lonely feeling is that by being married they are condemned to talking only to ugly women. This is a sweeping statement, but with the basis of truth in it. *Viz.*, a husband is home late from the office and tells his wife that he bumped into Liz and he had a drink with her. (The wife already knows this, anyway, having had a phone call from a fellow-member of the Women's Union who had observed the occurrence.) "Oh, yes?" says his wife. "And how's Liz? Etc., etc." All is well. Because Liz, a brilliant young woman, intelligent, successful, stimulating to talk to, fun to be with, is ugly. But if Liz, besides all those conversational good things, is beautiful, then stopping off for a drink with her, having a chat in a quiet corner of the patio at a party or whatever the circumstances may be—down comes the curtain with a bang on that one. So, doomed to seek the company only of unattractive women, the average husband can get mighty lonely for the enjoyment of being with a good-looking woman who is stimulating to talk to—that whole category is ruled out for him the instant he puts a ring on a third finger, for any wife is convinced that there is only one reason why her husband would wish to have an animated chat with such as they.

But we are concerned here primarily with the single person, and the way our society has evolved it seems especially designed to produce loneliness. The singles bars and other present-day efforts to allow girls to circulate freely have made only a slight dent on the problem. The commune and other aspects of the permissive brand of our society have as yet made no detectable difference to the general life of everyday people.

In the country and the small town, lonely beings proliferate through the terrible shortage of new faces and the way things have developed in the big city, although there are lots of people around, there is the ever present stumbling block that it is "not done" to strike up conversation with a stranger of the opposite sex except in certain prescribed circumstances. In day-to-day situations—going to the office, at the shopping center, etc.—no matter how attracted one might be by the sight of someone of the opposite sex, one cannot rush up to him or her and start talking.

If a man should do it he is running the risk of an embarrassing setback in front of everybody. Highly strung women have been known to scream, fighting for their honor when it is not even at stake.

If a woman should do it, there is the stigma of her being on the make, if not on the streets.

So regulated has our public behavior become that only the boldest of persons will cut across these strictures.

But here's the interesting thing. Convention has laid down that the city dweller must abide by these rules—but only when on home territory. The moment he or she is on the move, takes train, plane, ship, or whatever it may be away from the regular environment, then it is quite different. The girl who wouldn't dream of talking to you on a crosstown bus will talk to you on a Greyhound.

Why is this? Why is it that when moving to a new locale or on arrival there it is considered perfectly all right for members of the opposite sex who are strangers to each other to burst into spontaneous conversation? Walk up to that attractive woman in the lobby of a New York hotel and start talking to her and there could be trouble. Change the setting to a resort hotel, and no trouble at all.

The thing is that they have something in common. Not like

the bank clerk, say, and the fashion model coming from work in the city and trumped-up conversation starters have to be brought into play, such as asking the time or seeking street directions. They have a common topic of conversation, staying at the same hotel on a holiday, or both on this train to Chicago or whatever diversion from their humdrum daily lives they may be experiencing at the same time.

But of course the underlying reason for either party to have no hesitation in making an approach and to be receptive is that travel, a change of scene, heightens sex. When you make a move your whole being is stimulated, you're getting out of your regular rut, there's a sense of excitement. For example, it is an oft-repeated pattern that when a long-married couple whose take-it-or-leave-it attitude toward the marriage bed comes down heavily on the side of leave-it go on holiday they are no sooner in that double bed with the sound of the waves swishing on the beach outside than all of a sudden they are Don Juan and Cleopatra.

Which is all very well. But the bulk of people are not traveling all the time and invariably go on vacation but once a year. Which leaves us back with the original problem of young men holding off in fear of a rebuff and girls hesitating because they do not wish to appear forward, that sad situation of the girl bursting at the seams to have some particular man talk to her and she must just watch him walk away.

And a girl doesn't need to be unattractive to achieve this sort of thing. A beautiful girl can be among the loneliest of them all. For two reasons. First, because girl friends can steer clear of her, on the basis that she is so good-looking that they don't wish to be shown up by comparison and don't wish to miss out because male attention always gravitates toward the one who is a knockout. And second, many males who she would like very much to do something about her shy away because they feel that they just don't have a chance. Many extremely beautiful women can be found to be sexually naive, due to this avoidance through the years.

I don't think it is for us here to go into the numerous ways the gap can be bridged, since Julius Fast, in his book *Body Language*, has devoted considerable wordage to the subject and any girl can find there advice about how to get to meet that interesting looking man. Such as, for example, the type who will stand against the mantel and "lock his thumbs in his belt right above the pockets and his fingers will point down to his genitals . . . the obvious and effective signal . . . 'I am all man and I want you!' " Whether she in turn wants a man who locks his thumbs in his belt and points his fingers down to his genitals is something a girl must decide for herself.

The only thing I would add to the Fast observations is this simple piece of advice to the lonely girl: Get a dog.

The dog, which not without reason has earned the title of man's best friend, has probably brought more people together than any other single catalyst. If a girl takes a dog out she will find that men will have no hesitation in talking to her.

"That's a wonderful looking dog you've got there. What's his name?"

"Actually it's a she."

(Laughter.)

And off they launch into conversation, on the safe basis of the camaraderie of dog lovers, from which anything can develop. And the beauty of it is that she can be choosy, giving the freeze to any dog admirer she doesn't like the look of.

That's all very well, you may say, but for a working girl living in a room—the very type who *are* lonely—it isn't practical to own a dog. You can easily get around that.

I remember in my youth having a stay in the south of Spain and meeting, through her dog, a local girl of rare beauty. We both happened to be spectators at a tennis tournament and there was this cute little wirehaired terrier pup . . . "Just like one we used to have, my family have always had wirehaireds" . . . etc., etc. There followed the colorful splendor of bullfights shared, the strumming of Spanish guitars under a mellow Mediterranean moon, all that sort of thing. So caught up was I in the thrall of it all that a full week had elapsed before it suddenly occurred to me: What the hell ever happened to that dog of hers? Borrowed, of course. And having done its duty it was not needed any more.

So, lonely one, borrow a dog. There are dozens of dog owners in any given area only too glad of your offer to take it for a walk. "Prince" could change the whole pattern of your life.

It must be admitted, however, that much of the blame for the big romance that never gets off the ground must lie with the male, particularly in regard to that vital moment in any new male-female association—when the first pass is made.

Those men who take sex in their stride need not bother to read on from here, since at this juncture we are not concerned with them. We are referring to a large proportion of males, who are nice guys, the sort the average girl fancies much in preference to the eager beavers, but who could be much more helpful about the whole thing. Time and again they withhold that first pass—through shyness, fear of a rebuff, doubts whether they have correctly read the situation and it is in fact "on." And so long do they hold back that, reluctantly, the girl sees it all go begging, he winds up with somebody else, because she had been placed in a dilemma: perhaps he really doesn't want to do anything about me and if *I* take the initiative I could look an awful fool.

In an effort to ease the situation all round, I would offer young men what I feel are four helpful hints in regard to Making the Pass.

Timing

This is just a short, sharp piece of advice that many males ignore merely through ignorance of the feminine syndrome. Never ever make that first pass at a girl who is all dressed up to go out—new hairdo, makeup painstakingly applied, etc. She won't thank you for it. Here she is, all ready for the big evening out with you, she's spent *hours* ensuring that she will

look her best—and you go and mess the whole goddam thing
up.

The Partial Pass

This really comes under the heading of testing the feeling
of the meeting. The situation has arisen whereby you feel
you should move in. But you're not quite sure. Maybe you'll
get the ego-deflating, "You're awfully nice, I like you im-
mensely, you're great fun to be with, BUT . . ." The simple
solution is to try things out with the Partial Pass—make
physical contact in an innocent way and deduce from her
reaction whether or not she would be averse to escalation in
that area. There are numerous opportunities for this. Admire
a ring she is wearing. Take her arm crossing a street. At the
window admiring the night sky at the end of late work at the
office, put an arm around her shoulder, after all it's a twenty-two story drop and you're just being protective.

This might seem so obvious as to be not worthy of mention but girls will bear out that there are a surprising number
of shy young men who keep themselves resolutely at arm's
length. What it is, of course, is that it is so much on their
minds, they are so tensed up about the prospect of bodily
delights that they feel that any sort of physical contact, no
matter how innocent, will be construed as attempted rape.

The Verbal Pass

This is foolproof. It is by far the most intelligent approach
to the situation. Thus:

"Harold, why have you gone so quiet all of a sudden?"

"I'm just sitting here thinking how attractive you are and
wondering what your reaction would be if I kissed you."

Excellent. There is no likelihood of embarrassment on
either side; no chance of a loss of pride for the man through a
physical rebuff, no necessity for the girl to have to think of
how to cope with unwanted grappling.

The ball is neatly lobbed into her court and it is simple for
her to return it in one of two ways. Either she smiles sweetly
and says: "Why don't you try it?" Or there is a chilly, "I
don't think you'd find it very rewarding."

Either way, the thing is brought to a head and moves at once on to a take-it-from-there basis.

The Dive Pass

To be avoided at all costs, this is something that occurs all too frequently. Nothing much has really developed yet, on account of you're the bashful sort and she's pretty tentative herself. But then there comes an evening when the setting is right. And what are you up to? You're talking about electronics or the place of plastics in today's world or whatever happens to be your field and you continue banging the poor girl's ear for three quarters of an hour or so. And then, all of a sudden, quite out of the blue, in mid-sentence, you make a dive at her. Okay, so you were nervous about plucking up the courage to do it. But a dive pass like that! You're likely to scare a girl right out of her wits.

The paradoxical thing is that we must be thankful for loneliness, for without it life would be terrible, almost impossible to live. For this reason: Loneliness has much in common with memory. On the face of it, this may seem an odd link, but here is the point I would make. What is astounding about memory is not that we are capable of remembering so many things—from something embarrassing that happened at school years upon years ago to a joke we heard last week—but, our amazing ability *not* to remember things. If the part of our brain which controls memory were called upon to record every single thing we saw and heard every hour of every day, month after month, year after year, the sheer burden of having to carry all those things in our minds would drive us crazy. Anyone who has a nervous breakdown has an inkling of this—the racing through the mind of all sorts of things which normally one keeps under control, pigeonholed in a corner of the mind to be called upon if and when required.

What, you may well ask, has this got to do with loneliness? Just this: No one is completely without friends and associates, but the Lonely Ones want more, far more, of them. But supposing one were to live in a state which would be the antithesis of loneliness. Supposing you knew *everybody*. Just imagine it. You would not be able to move out of your home without having to stop every few yards to talk to one of your myriad friends. Your phone would never stop ringing. You would never be able to cope with all the letters you would be getting. The calls on you for lovemaking alone would be such that that in itself would be a full-time job.

Trying to keep up with it, like trying to retain in one's memory every single thing one experiences, would drive us out of our minds. Fortunately, just as our memories are selective, there are barriers against our having so many friends, social and intimate, that we can't keep up with the situation. Such barriers as shyness, the necessity to conform to convention, introversion, different social status, and so on.

On balance, it is far better that things are the way they are.

The Woman Executive

She wears the black dress—the "basic" black dress as women call it. It is beautifully cut and immaculately fitting. Underneath it is the well-engineered foundation garment, giving her what she feels is the correctly contoured bosom, stomach, and posterior—although men, of course, would much prefer her to give indication of having breasts and buttocks. Her nylons are impeccable, her shoes "correct." She turns on what she feels is just the appropriate amount of rehearsed vivacity and feminine charm, and then hastens to assume the wrinkled brow of concentration and serious mien when the Big Decision is under discussion.

She is, as somebody once brilliantly put it, the Steel Marshmallow.

They are wonderful to watch in action, these women. They are acting, of course, all the time. It is the Important Executive bit and their whole makeup, attire, and behavior is attuned to demonstrating that they fit snugly into the whole man's world of the boardroom and the executive suite.

But apart from the feminine sound effects which they

keep giving out—the clanking of chunky jewelry, the scrape of cross-legged nylons—there is something else which men who work close to them cannot help but notice. It is a particular aroma that cuts right through just that suggestion of perfume which they allow themselves on the executive level. It is certainly not B.O., because that would be unthinkable in the woman executive. It is a vaguely pelvic odor which a man cannot help but be conscious of when he gets together with Miss Highpower to study in detail the new figures from the sales department. It is not distasteful nor is it pleasantly evocative, but it is unmistakably feminine.

Now, the thing I learn about this is that although men are fully aware of it, women will tell you that it does not actually exist. When the matter came up during a discussion I had with a woman psychiatrist she said: "It is purely in men's imagination. The point is that a woman in an important position represents a challenge to male superiority. To reduce that challenge in his mind he imputes to her the giving out of some essentially feminine aroma so that he can be reminded that despite her apparent efficiency she is after all just a woman and won't be able to get as far in the firm as he'll be able to."

Interesting, if true.

Childbirth

A thing which women constantly throw at men is that they have a far greater capacity to withstand pain. This is usually brought up when a man is feeling sorry for himself with a minor ailment such as a cold or a stiff neck. This gives women the opportunity to say: "You men are such babies when you have the least thing wrong with you. I'd like to see you go through childbirth. You'd never be able to stand up under it!" This familiar feminine sally is an argument that can never be resolved. It is not given to men to undertake the bearing of children, so there is no way of knowing how they would grapple with it. In the same way there is no way of judging how women would stand up under the tremendous amounts of pain, often over sustained periods, that men have to endure in war.

Something which women do not seem to bear in mind when they are sounding off about childbirth is that it is not an illness, disease, or ailment of any sort. It is not a terrible physical misfortune that has suddenly befallen them. It is a perfectly natural thing which the female body is specially designed to cope with. And to help them through it all there are on hand, doctors, midwives, and nurses specifically trained to ease things for them in their time of travail. By comparison, what of the poor bastard who has a leg blown off out in the middle of nowhere in war, lying there without any medics yet available, no one to give him a shot of something to put him out when the agony is at its height? Given the choice of such as that or childbirth, wouldn't any man opt to have a go at childbirth?

Often when I hear a woman who is on about the childbirth bit I think of a young man I knew called George. George was a "basket case."

He was in the navy on convoy duty in sub-zero weather. When his ship was torpedoed he was taken from the water hours later and his body bundled into a basket, written off. But George was determined to live. On innumerable visits to hospital, where doctors broke the bones of his arms and legs and reset them to straighten out his huddled body, the agonies he suffered may have been akin to the pain of childbirth. I know it lasted much longer. A matter of years.

I met George at a holiday resort, in his wheelchair pushed by the man who had "adopted" him. He was a local hotelier who had been in a bed beside George in hospital for a period and had felt so sorry for the young man who would never be able to look after himself again that he had suggested to his wife that they take him under their wing—a wonderfully unselfish act. They took him everywhere with them, on their walks to the beach or the harbor, visiting friends, to the bars and places of entertainment in the area. Everybody knew

George, of the alert eyes, quick mind and keen sense of humor. They called him "Cheerful George." His mind was the only part of his body that was fully alive. He could barely make any movement with his hands or legs. Everything had to be done for him. It was fascinating to watch when he smoked. Leonard, the hotelkeeper, had an uncanny knack of knowing precisely when the ash of the cigarette in George's mouth needed to be flicked off. Still chatting to whoever he was talking to, Leonard would reach his hand out from time to time for George to jerk his head down and tap the ash into it.

Once, when I was out with them, some experts at horse-shoe pitching were having an exciting match and I felt that George would be interested in watching it. I moved his wheel-chair, which was more like a mobile stretcher, so that he was turned around and could see the game. In a little while, after Leonard had rejoined us with some drinks, I noticed that George did not look his usual cheerful self. "What's wrong with George?" I asked Leonard. He smiled. "You shouldn't have moved him around. He was looking at that blonde over there. I knew he thought she was terrific, because his toes were twitching."

Poor guy, I felt. Shortly after this he returned for another period in hospital. More pain to endure.

I don't know. Perhaps women do, as they claim, have greater fortitude when it comes to coping with physical suffering. But the existence of George and many others like him would seem to indicate that women have a rather one-sided, distorted view of the matter.

Daughter Animosity

Despite all the publicity about the Generation Gap, despite the efforts of the Women's Libbers to break up the family unit, families in vast numbers throughout the world continue to behave like normal families. And something perfectly normal, but worrying at the time, is a problem that besets the father with a daughter in her teens.

"We just don't get on as well together as we used to."

This lament long predates the relatively modern invention of "the teen-ager" as a quite separate group of beings as distinct as toddlers and senior citizens. The worry on the part of the father is that he had such fun with his daughter when she was a little girl. They got on like a house afire together. Then all of a sudden she turns against him. He is hurt that not only does she not seek his company but displays downright animosity toward him. The years of her teens become agony to him, his failure to get across to her, to assuage, no matter how hard he tries, the dislike she so obviously shows toward him. What has he done to warrant it? Nothing that he can think of.

One is always meeting men in the throes of daughter animosity. At time of writing I know one man who gets along fine with his teen-age son but is absolutely at his wits' end in regard to his two daughters. I know another who has gone to the extent of breaking with his wife, because he thinks that his daughter's belligerence toward him is something initiated by the mother. He should have waited, for all would have come right in the end.

The point to remember about this whole thing is that it has been going on for generation after generation and, as we shall see, it is just as well that it has. The psychological explanation is quite simple, and those fathers fortunate enough to know what it stems from can ride it through, even though they would much prefer not having to.

One does not have to be a psychiatrist to know that a child falls in love, spiritually not sexually, with the first person of the opposite sex it gets to know well—*i.e.*, the boy with his mother and the girl with her father. Elsewhere we go into the son-mother association, which does not have a hatred period similar to that inflicted on a father by his daughter, but we are concerned here with the girl.

Everything is fine when he is buying her dolls and delivering her to a party in her new "stick-out" party frock and taking her to a theater for her first wondrous glimpse of *Copelia*. She revels in the close association with the sense of masculine strength, the smell of pipe smoke, and the feel of rough suiting, as a welcome change from the aura of feminine softness with which her mother surrounds her. But then in her personal development comes the awareness of sex and, although it is purely subconscious and she probably doesn't even know of the word's existence, the prospect of incest presents itself. Her natural instinct is to be revolted by this and to put from her the person who represents this threat. So father is banished, as far as she is concerned, not because she has thought this thing out and decided that that is the way it must be, but purely instinctively.

The reason why, in the usual family, she is back with her father on a harmonious basis when she reaches her twenties (and what joy it is to a man when this happens) is that she has by then entered into perfectly normal sexual relationships with boyfriends and it is safe to return to closeness with the man who, subconsciously, loomed up as an abnormal association.

I said that it is just as well that this is so and the best way to illustrate this is to tell of the case of a girl we shall call Joan.

She was an airline stewardess and a good one, as evidenced by the fact that when she came up to the age limit for stewardesses (ever noticed you never have an *old* stewardess on a plane, since the airlines feel it is psychologically better to have them young and beautiful), when she came to this fateful age they said they would keep her on as an instructress. This was fair enough but nevertheless a reminder that she was getting on in years—and unmarried. She had the normal desire to have children and all the other feminalia. But the trouble was that the man she loved was married. He was, of course, an airline pilot, since it is an occupational hazard for stewardesses to be impressed by the so-called glamour, which other people find easy to resist, of the airborne bus drivers.

Max was from, shall we say, Cleveland. Married, three children. When he was in New York waiting to fly out he would live with Joan. When, happily, they were assigned to the same flight they would share the pleasures of London, Paris, or the beaches of some exotic spot on the map. As the affair progressed Joan, with apparently the natural feminine inclination to put it on a more firm basis, went to the wife in Cleveland and asked her to give Max a divorce so that she could marry him. Not on your life, said Max's wife. She knew all about the love nest in New York and the goings-on in distant places, but if it wasn't with Joan it would be with somebody else so one should not get too worked up about it. When Max was in Cleveland she had her homelife with him and the children and that was satisfactory enough. Did Joan really expect her to agree to divorce Max and throw herself on the marriage market, a divorced woman with the encumbrance of three young children? Oh, no.

So there was the situation. The wife, if not happy, was levelheaded enough to come to terms with the way things stood. Max was as happy as a mudlark, with the pleasures of family life to enjoy when he was at home, with a regular roll in the hay laid on in New York, plus all the comforts lavished upon him by Joan *and* was able to pocket the full amount of the airline's New York living allowance which he did not have to outlay. And the only one who wasn't getting a fair shake was poor Joan.

It worried my wife and me to see an attractive young woman wasting her life in this way, the thing dragging on and the passage of years starting to drop hints in her appearance. She was leaving it rather late if Max turned elsewhere and she had to start from scratch again finding a husband. So we were at pains to bring her into the company of eligible young men. We could arouse no interest from her in any of them. Max was her shining light.

One evening she was at a party we gave and also present was a psychiatrist brought along by a doctor friend of ours. We had met the psychiatrist a couple of times and my wife used to say of him, jokingly but with the nub of truth: "I don't like being with him. I always feel naked when he's around."

He was indeed perceptive and during the course of the evening we happened to mention to him that we were concerned about Joan and told him that we had been trying to find another man for her.

"You're wasting your time," he said. "Unless, of course, it's another married man."

"Why do you say that?" my wife asked.

"She has a father complex."

"How do you know?" I said. "You've hardly talked to her."

"You don't need to talk to her a lot to realize that."

"Come to think of it," said my wife, "she *is* always talking about her father back at home, always saying what a wonderful person he is."

Our psychiatrist friend nodded. "She's in love with him. So—every man she takes up with has to be like her father. Unavailable, somebody she can't have."

"She *has* told me about other men, before Max," said my wife. "They were all married men."

"Of course. She'll go on repeating the pattern. In ten years time she could wind up in the loony bin."

I have never met Joan's father. It is probable that he feels that it is great that always, from the word go, without break, he has had this warm affectionate relationship with his daughter. Such as he perhaps feel a certain superiority over men they hear complaining about daughter animosity. "It has never happened to me, thank heaven." But heaven is not to be thanked. Any father should know that daughter animosity in those formative years of her life, although hard for him to take at the time, is much preferable to having one of those unhappy souls, the Joans of this world, the girls with a father complex.

8   WELCOME ON THE MAT

Some time ago I had occasion to be sitting with a group of men friends in the Embassy Room of the Windsor Hotel in Montreal. We were having a few drinks and chatting when I noticed an attractive young woman making her way between the tables, obviously on her way to the powder room. She was so good looking that I was prompted to say something to her as she passed.

"Hello, there!" I said. "How are you?"

She stopped and looked at me, as though trying to establish recognition.

"Good to see you again," I said, inaccurately. "What are you doing in Montreal?"

"I've come up for the skiing," she said. "I'm going to Mont Tremblant."

"Ah, good!" I said. "Mont Tremblant is great. You can take the ski tow up to the top of the mountain, ski down, and there at the bottom there's a cocktail waiting for you."

"Oh, yes?" she said. "But is there a cock waiting for me?"

Thus, unexpectedly, one encounters from time to time the nymphomaniac.

I have now confronted myself with a small problem, of the type which often crops up for those of us who write both novels and books of nonfiction. I could go on to describe what happened after that chance meeting, the chain of events which beside being fast-moving and absorbing for any student of human nature was also not without its comedy element. But the novelist in me knows that not only would it make a

very good set piece for the new novel but also that young
lady, whom I was to learn was of a good Boston family, had
so many interesting facets that she would build into an intriguing character for that book. So, if you don't mind, I would
rather save her for that.

After the initial heightening of interest, when shortly the
locale moved from the Embassy Room to a less public place,
there was to be seen the familiar male tendency to back away
from the nymphomaniac. The point is that when the chips
are down the average male shies away. In youth one thinks
how wonderful it would be to have a nymphomaniac—a glorious release from the tussles, the arguments, the frustration of
sexual interplay with the girls one knows when growing up. I
always remember the comment of a friend of my youth:
"I'm not going to get married. I'm going to live in sin with a
nymphomaniac who can cook."

But when one does encounter nymphomania one finds
that it doesn't measure up to one's youthful estimate. And
later in life one cannot help but be made aware of it, ranging
from the attractive New York socialite who in the gloom of a
nightclub cannot resist the urge to be under the table turning
on her own particular type of floor show to the well-known
lady of the entertainment world who comes off the stage or
from the film set and buttonholes the nearest stagehand, elec-
trician, any man, with the entreaty, "For God's sake put it
into me." Such blatant invitations, freely distributed to one
and all, may find ready acceptance with some. The bulk of
men however are intrigued but hesitant.

In the first place there is no sense of conquest, which is
such an important component of man's enjoyment of sex. To
have strived and achieved is flattering to the male ego. Merely
to avail oneself of the available is as flat as beating your rival
at some game when in the back of your mind you sense he
has let you beat him.

Second, by the very fact that she is a nymphomaniac, the
woman is promiscuous. This offends a man's sensibilities. The

average man has a basic respect for womanhood and, although condoning it in himself, tends to frown on promiscuity in its female manifestation. And in this regard, even more pressing on his mind, is the reality that if he has sexual intercourse with a nymphomaniac he might get more than he bargained for.

And finally, which is an unhappy thing for them, nymphomaniacs are soon found by men to be a bore.

A young man my wife and I knew had an extremely good-looking girl friend. Not only was she what could justifiably be called a knockout, but she had loads of animation and we were pleased for him that the girl he would in due course marry had that happy admixture of good looks and personality. But he dropped out of our acquaintance for a time and when we saw him again he was not with that girl from whom he had formerly been inseparable.

"It's all off," he confided in me. "Nymphomaniacs become such a bore. All right, it was great, the bed part of it. But she would never give it a rest. Whenever we were out she would be forever undoing my shirt and sliding her hand in or when we were sitting down leaning on my leg with her elbow right up into me. It was not only embarrassing in front of everybody but it got so tedious. I couldn't have a good discussion with somebody about our work or have an argument about the big game without her mauling me all the time."

There were other aspects, such as whenever he was going out of town for a while on business he had to extract a promise from her that she would do her best to be discriminating about the company she kept during his absence. But apart from this revelation about this girl whom we thought was going to be his wife, there was something else that interested me.

It crystallized in my mind the fact that men don't like women who behave like men.

For in all honesty I had to admit that all she had been doing is what men do all the time. Her availability in bed was merely the parallel of men's eagerness to have sex very frequently; her inability to keep her hands off our young friend when out and about was typical male behavior.

The enjoinder, "Oh, *please*," so often heard by men from women cannot be so lightly regarded when it comes home to roost—when it is the *man* who is in the position of having to give voice to it.

9   "I'LL HAVE THE SAME, PLEASE"

Most graffiti is not worth reading, being either just plain crude or as hackneyed as "Merry Christmas to All Our Readers." But occasionally there is the glimmer of wit, as in the example I remember seeing in one public convenience. On the wall was, "My mother made me a homosexual," and underneath it someone had written, "If I send her the wool, will she make me one, too?"

Much has been written, more seriously, about the train of homosexuals that mother-domination is said to leave in its wake. At school one feels sorry for the boy who has been turned into a sissy by his mother. The young man who says to his friend that it is a waste of time chasing after skirt, why not just enjoy their own company? And saddest sight of all, the aging queer. "I promised Mother I would never marry while she was still alive." And Mother clings stubbornly to life. . . .

But seeing this over and again I remember what a doctor once wisely said to me: "It is not what happens to you that makes you what you are. It's how you take it."

I was very much dominated by my mother. I got out from under. That was how I took it, like many another man who has done likewise. But the latent homosexual *wants* to be dominated by his mother.

In my case I got so far away that I was out of reach. But other men do not always find that that is practical. Often the situation has to be dealt with in other ways. For instance, there is one of our leading television entertainers, unmarried, who is in the position that his mother was of great help to him in his getting where he is, denying herself much so that he could further his ambition. He owes her a great debt. She will not let him forget that. Widowed now, she demands that much of his spare time be devoted to her. Result of this is that whenever one picks up a newspaper he seems to be pictured with a new girl, with whom he is "just good friends." An acid-tongued woman remarked to him: "Really, you should change the sheets between girl friends." There is some question as to whether that is actually necessary. What he more correctly can be said to be doing is using what the psychiatrists call the "Look, Mom, I'm free of you," technique. For a latent homosexual, he is putting up a fairly good fight.

The point is that a dominating mother doesn't turn her son into a homosexual. If he wants to be a homosexual he will go right ahead and be one. She is not the deciding factor, as evidenced by the thousands upon thousands of sons who have had dominating mothers and it did not in the least deter them from their ardent desire to be heterosexual.

I think of that doctor's axiom that it is not what happens to you in life but how you take it that makes you what you are when, for instance, I hear someone say of a drunk: "He's a decent fellow, really. You can't honestly blame him. He lost his wife and his business failed through no real fault of his." Many men have lost their wives or have gone bankrupt but it doesn't make them alcoholics. The person in question had a character fault which prevented him from being able to stand up to setbacks. If it were not the setbacks mentioned it would be some other thing which would give him the excuse to seek in the bottle an escape from reality.

Likewise with homosexuals: "You can't really blame him, the way that mother of his has had him tied to her apron strings all his life." The man tied to his mother's apron strings who didn't sever them didn't really want to.

Homosexuals are born, not made (except for those fringe types in show business and elsewhere where there is so much opportunity for the normal that some turn to the abnormal for kicks). You cannot "cure" a homosexual. As easily force a dyed-in-the-wool heterosexual to be homosexual.

But since women form the subject of this book, we are not concerned with dealing in depth with the male homosexual. Our only interest is the degree of feminine influence. And it must be admitted that in certain respects female domination *is* capable of causing disaster.

In the city where I spent much of my youth there was a well-known local citizen whom we shall call Taylor. He had made a lot of money out of real estate, was highly respected in the community, a member of the local council, served on numerous committees and so on. He lived with his large family in a palatial home in extensive grounds, as befitted his stature as a public figure. Adjoining his estate was the school I attended for a time and so large was his property that boys living on the other side of it had the choice of a long, round-about trip to and from school or taking a shortcut through his woods. Naturally they chose the latter.

At school there started to be whispering among the boys about certain goings-on in the woods. It seemed that Mr. Taylor was stopping certain of the boys on their trips across his property, not to reprimand them for trespassing, but to chat with them. Gossip had it that on more than one occasion Mr. Taylor had been what might be termed over-friendly. Since there was nothing sinister about Mr. Taylor the average well-adjusted boy usually regards such things as pretty much of a joke to be shared among his chums. But it came to the notice of parents, mainly because of presents some of the boys were getting from Mr. Taylor. One parent went to the police. Statements were taken and the police decided they would pay a call on Mr. Taylor, discreetly, in view of his position in the community.

The call never took place. Clearly Taylor had become aware of the police investigations. A big headline in our afternoon paper told of the suicide of this important figure in civic affairs. It has always stayed vividly in my mind because of the undignified and public way in which he had chosen to do it. On the previous night he had driven to the end of one of the wharves in the harbor and taken from the car a large rock to which a rope had been attached. This he tied around his neck and jumped into the water.

Being young at the time I just went along with the general comment that, "after all these years it's come out that Taylor was a queer." I heard grown-ups saying: "But what about the fact that he had a family?" And those who wanted to give the impression of being knowledgeable about such things pronouncing sagely: "You can be both, you know."

But later in life, thinking about it, I reached my own conclusion. I didn't think for one moment that Taylor had been a homosexual, although he knew only too well that everybody would think he was, and that was why he had taken his own life.

The reason I felt that way was this: his family consisted of six daughters. This plethora of feminine offspring had given rise to many a ribald remark behind his back about what had obviously been his concerted efforts to have a son, but clearly it had been no joke to him. Poor man. A six-time trip through the world of birthday and Christmas presents for girls. The dolls, the nurse's outfit, cookery set, the first party frock, dresses, makeup kit, dresses. Gifts a man buys in consultation with his wife, the "you just get it and say it's from me" sort of presents. Taking girls to the ballet and endless Sound-of-Music movies, never a football game or an "action-packed story of wartime heroism." Never the fun of buying boys' presents. The first penknife, cowboy holster, train set, baseball glove, the Rapid Firing Death Ray Disintegrator. I had never heard any of the boys who took the shortcut through the Taylor property give any specific details of anything terrible that had happened. When a father affectionately puts his arm around his son's shoulders, that's O.K., but if the boy isn't his son, watch it, chum.

Among the numerous reasons why homosexuality is more prevalent with females than males is the fact that the laws of so many countries around the world have long been indulgent toward the lesbian, while coming down heavily on the male equivalent. Despite a certain easing recently of this discrimination against men, the general situation is that whereas two women making love to each other commit no legal offense, male dalliance features prominently on the statute books.

A basic reason why this should be so is that as far as women are concerned, their physical equipment is such that there really isn't much that the dears can do to one another, in contrast to the bodily makeup of the more forceful male. Kate Millett, in her *Sexual Politics* deals lingeringly, for page after page with male homosexuality but dismisses lesbianism merely with a footnote, presumably because of what she calls "the more explosive (because more realistically conceived) topic of male homosexuality."

On the same basis that there is much more drinking where the consumption of alcoholic beverages is legal than where it isn't, women have naturally taken advantage of their immunity from the law. They are by nature anyway much more inclined to be demonstrative about showing their affection for one another than are men—that empathy of theirs which the feminists are so fond of telling us they have to a much greater degree. Also they are much more intimate in conversation among themselves, as dealt with elsewhere in this book. Life in the powder room is much cosier than in the men's room. Women linger. There are facilities for them to linger. I have yet to see an armchair in a men's lavatory. Women concern themselves with each other's bra problems and other things too luridly personal about their bodies to mention here. The whole aura of life among the girls is of an intimacy not paralleled by men and it is only natural that this can spill over into lesbianism, even if only on a tentative, experimental basis.

Your hard-core lesbian, however, is born to it and invariably she winds up a very unhappy soul because frustration is probably the greatest bugbear of lesbianism. As we have been discussing, the sexual pattern of women is quite different from that of men—which makes sense. It means that when the two are enjoined it works out fine. But to try to achieve the same sort of goal with two of the female side of the arrangement cannot help but be ultimately unsatisfactory. One of the underlying causes of this is the female capacity for multiple orgasm. When lesbians make love it goes on and on and on. The sequence is all wrong. There is no reaching of a supreme high point and subsequent fulfilled relaxation. Lesbians making love puts one in mind of the sort of review one has read many a time of a new musical that has just opened on Broadway. The tunes are good, the lyrics ingenious, the sets attractive, the production numbers well-executed. But the whole thing lacks a show-stopper.

In an effort to remedy this they call into use a variety of gadgets, some of which require putting a pan of milk on the stove, which would seem to be a rather prosaic way of bringing that famous female empathy to the boil. Male reaction to this use of complicated gadgetry is why go to all that trouble when I'm here ready, willing, and self-equipped? But it is usually unwise at any time to attempt to interpose, since the active, butch member of the partnership can turn very nasty. Violent, even, as more than one man has found when, quite innocently, he has engaged a personable young lady in conversation, only to find that she is merely waiting for the return from the powder room of her "friend" who arrives on the scene eyes blazing.

The unhappy lot of the lesbian extends to her economic situation. It is almost always more advantageous financially for two males to set up their own little household. When two men share an apartment together they are pooling two male salaries and this means that they are living on two pay checks that are much better than the combined pay of two lesbians living together. That is why you invariably find that in a pansy household they are doing very well indeed, well furnished, all sorts of luxuries, because not only do they have their two male salaries combined but also, with no such thing as children, they have nothing to do but spend their money on themselves. Over on the other side, however, lower female pay like as not has lesbians living in a pretty squalid setup, often made even worse by the fact that the butch of the partnership insists on being the wage earner while the femme stays at home and keeps house, bringing in no money at all.

You may be sure, though, that the Women's Liberationists are looking into this unfair male-female balance and although, as with so many physiological disadvantages of the female, there is nothing they can do to improve that side of it for the lesbian, they can at least try to achieve for her financial equality with the male homosexual.

10   SOMETHING LACKING

It is difficult for anyone writing on the subject of penis envy to resist the temptation to start by telling the story of the girl on the school outing who went behind the bushes and, finding young Johnny there on the same errand, said: "That's a handy little gadget to have on a picnic."

There is no question that possession of a penis affords the male certain advantages over the female. What boy living in a cold climate has not written his name in the snow—or at least his initials, depending on how great his need at the time. The penis is something with which one can be demonstrative. I remember a man whom we shall call H. He was of humble background but by diligent application he had managed to do well for himself as a building contractor. A *femme fatale* who had run out of husbands and who had reached the stage when there was more in bulk of the *femme* than there was of the *fatale* took H. under her wing. He was flattered, because even though she was aging she had what was to him the sort of class he had never attained, and it was a useful arrangement as far as she was concerned because he could finance her drinking. Not only her own drinking but also that of her friends and associates. They were a familiar sight, those two, in the drinking places of the area where I was living at the time—she holding court at the bar and ordering innumerable rounds of drinks and H. paying up when instructed. Nobody ever talked to H. because, having tried, they found that there was no conversation; he was out of his depth socially and intellectually. I always felt sorry for him, standing off by himself, unspoken to, saying nothing, just sipping his drink and digging deep into his wallet when told to by the duchess. The men's room at one of the places they frequented was in a courtyard behind the bar and one evening when I went out I saw H. standing there alone. He was peeing all over the white-washed walls of the courtyard in one glorious shower and saying, "Fuck 'em all!"

It was the longest sentence I had ever heard from him and I felt that it was a very apt capsule comment on the situation in which he found himself. It is not given to women to be able to be so explicit in such a spectacular way.

I know that what a man does standing up and a woman has to do squatting down is not what the psychiatrists are on about when they let themselves loose on their favorite topic of penis envy. They concern themselves with what they feel are much more profound considerations. No mention ever seems to be made of the difference in performance of the prosaic bodily function, but I feel that it cannot help but have a day in-day out psychological effect on the less happily equipped female. In the animal world it is vividly contrasted.

Observe your dog when you take it for a walk. If it is a male, even a mutt of the most obscure origin, see the jaunty air with which it lifts its leg at the nearest tree, looking around to review the situation out-of-doors as it gives the benefit of a pretty superior outpouring to those that are to follow. But if it is a bitch—see it squat there embarrassingly in the middle of the sidewalk with that moony look on its face as the miniature lake spreads out beneath it.

Humans are naturally less blatant about such things but it cannot help but contribute to the female feeling of inferiority that men can stand there with a casual, throw-away gesture, a minimum of their clothing disarranged, while a woman must always make a little performance of it, must assume an undignified, vulnerable posture, with clothing distastefully disarrayed.

It has all sorts of ramifications, all of them to the disadvantage of women. A delightful, typically English aspect concerns cricket. This game, once described as "baseball played in a coma," has matches of very long duration, anything up to six hours a day for five days, but the ardent fan never wants to miss a moment of it. Accordingly, not only are the bars situated in such a way that the game can be followed even while drinking, but with the sort of thoughtfulness for which the English are famous, the cricket authorities, when planning the main grandstand at the famous Lord's Cricket Ground in London saw to it that in the men's lavatory there is a row of windows above the urinals. These windows command a splendid view of the field of play, so that it has been assured that no male fan is likely to miss seeing a vital phase of the game through having to go and debeer himself. Sad to say, no such facilities can be arranged for the sedentary female fans.

In regard to this aspect of penis envy, I know of only one example where it *can* be said that women enjoy a certain advantage. When researching a piece I was writing on marathon swimmers, I came upon the incidental bit of information that your female marathon swimmer just keeps on going while that matter is looked after; the male swimmer has no option but to lose valuable time by stopping and treading water at such times.

However, because marathon swimming is something which comes within the scope of only a very small proportion of females, it is no great solace to them as a whole to learn that that is the way things go during the long haul across the English Channel or from one shore of Lake Ontario to the other.

But I can well understand why the psychiatrists, the writers for Women's Lib, and others who dwell at length on penis envy give such little houseroom to the urinary side of it. One reason is that even in today's permissive society, for us of the English-speaking peoples (as against those French and others who have no shame about it), it is still very much a taboo subject, one of bad taste. And the other reason, of course, is that it is far more interesting and makes for much higher reader demand if one gets on to the sex aspect of penis envy.

There seems no doubt that with phallic worship having been around for so many, many years, women should feel somewhat embittered about their own equipment.

The Romans of course contributed much of the aggrandizement of the penis. One can see every indication of this if one goes to the ruins of Pompeii, a most rewarding place to visit, since rather than just seeing what's left of one abbey, say, or a single castle, one can see the remains of a whole city—its streets, houses, shops, public buildings, whorehouses, etc.—and from it gain a very good idea of the way of life there 2,000 years, and more, ago.

In what had been the palatial residence of a well-to-do Roman whose interests included orgies, the mood is set for those visiting his home by a wall painting in the entrance lobby. Today the mural is behind locked shutters that have been built across it and when these are unlocked to reveal what is behind, one sees depicted there a centurion with his penis projecting from the undertrappings of his uniform. Never, in modern times at any rate, has there been such a penis. Like a great log of wood it stretches out before him, its end resting on one side of a pair of balance scales. On the other side, clearly outweighed, is a sack of money—a graphic illustration of the Roman contention that the big prick was worth its weight in gold.

The painting being kept under lock and key until such times as its custodian sees fit to reveal it has nothing to do with its being kept from the eyes of the young and the demure. The plain fact of the matter is that he charges tourists so much a peek and year after year whoever has the *Penis Superbus* concession must really clean up financially.

But one should not get the impression that the lauding of the penis at Pompeii is only on this peep-show level. Wherever one goes in the streets it is very much in evidence. Carved on the stone drinking fountains, for example, it is to be seen on one side, *ad dextra*, in erection (good luck) and on the other, *ad sinistra*, in flaccid state (bad luck).

An airborne version, another "Winged Victory" of a sort, was in fact the emblem of pleasure-loving Pompeii, if one can believe the souvenir-sellers who display by the dozens the examples of the "Flying Penis," complete with wings and testicular undercarriage, in the form of watch fobs, key chains, and even items to add to your charm bracelet. Rather cute.

Right through to modern times the glorification of the penis ("the phallus is all," as Kate Millett puts it) has been such that from the time the psychoanalysts got hold of it they have been at pains to tell us how strongly entrenched it is in our subconscious. We have reached a situation now whereby a woman dare not look thoughtful while putting her foot into a shoe without psychiatrists saying that it is a manifestation of phallic worship—the insertion of the penis into an encompassing enclosure. If that is the case, then girls who work in shoestores must be the most emotionally disturbed of females.

It pervades our literature, as Kate Millett has dwelt with at such great length in her studies of D. H. Lawrence, Henry Miller, *et al.* But if one would read the best written story wholly devoted to phallic worship one should read "A Snake of One's Own" by John Steinbeck (first published by *Esquire*) which tells of a young woman going into a pet store that sells snakes and picking out one in a glass case which she buys. When the man in the store asks her how she wants to transport it home she says that she doesn't want to take it. "Just put a mouse in with it," she says. The rest I leave to the brilliant writing of Steinbeck.

I suppose it is only natural, with all this publicity the penis has been getting over the years, that women should feel slighted. But I think it has caused them to get a distorted view of the whole thing. They are now feeling so sorry for themselves for what they feel is the general attitude toward the genitals—male and female—that they are like the child who, because his brother comes in for high praise from his parents, gets to thinking that it means automatically that they hate *me*. The penis is praised, therefore *ipso facto* the female counterpart is something to be despised.

This has led to Germaine Greer stating that "the worst name anyone can be called is *cunt*." She goes on about how the female has given rise to terms of loathing and disgust. But I can't ever remember hearing one man say to another, "Don't be such a *breast*" or "Shut up! You're behaving like a *clitoris*." In this regard Greer is merely reflecting the feminine feeling of being hard done by. Certainly the word *cunt* is used as a term of derision. But does a man's chest swell with pride when he's called a *prick*? In the context of verbal abuse the words *cunt* and *prick* are completely interchangeable.

We men are the ones who should be complaining. Not only is *prick* a term just as derogatory as *cunt*, but what about our balls? People are always saying terrible things like, "*Balls* to you!," "Don't talk such *balls*," "You've made a complete *balls* of this whole thing." Apart from *cunt* (and its stablemate *twat*), women get off scot-free as far as the rest of their genitalia are concerned. Does a foreman ever berate a worker

by saying, "You've made a right *vagina* of this job." If we
behaved like women we would cry ourselves to sleep at night
bemoaning the fact that our balls have become such a subject
of derision, ridicule, and vilification.

Germaine Greer, in her role as the voice of the suffering
female, writes: "Cunt-hatred has survived in our civilization
in myriad small manifestations, most of which would be
steadily denied by the manifesters. The deep aversion for
beaver in pin-ups evinced by the selection of poses which
minimize the genital area is partly motivated by disgust for
the organ itself." This is just plain naive.

One might as well say that the reason why the bosom was
never fully exposed in pin-ups in the past was because of
nipple-hatred. The motivation, the one and only reason for
the pin-up poses which minimized what Greer calls *beaver*
was the police. Only to avoid having the law come knocking
at their doors were the photographers at such pains to ensure
legs-strictly-together poses and to airbrush away any pubic
hair that might happen to stray into camera range. In pictures
for the public gaze, that is. When taking nude shots for private viewing, what photographer ever had a "deep aversion
for *beaver*"?

The full naiveté of the Greer assertion is indicated by the
fact that with the coming out into the open of the nipples in
our modern permissive society it was only logical that pubic
hair, too, would come into its own. By 1971 even *Playboy*,
that purveyor of the antiseptic nude, was displaying the female pelvic area *au naturel*—a clear indication that it had
been pure and simple censorship, not cunt-hatred, that had
kept this region from the eyes of the pin-up viewers of yester-
year.

A great job could be done by the Women's Liberationists
in getting across to women that they really must stop feeling
so sorry for themselves in regard to that which is between
their legs. Women have succumbed to all those Freudian out-
pourings about the female child coming to the conclusion
that she's a castrated male.

Like reading a medical book and imagining one has all sorts of illnesses, women are being influenced by the findings of psychoanalysts who deal basically with females who are all mixed up anyway, whether penis envy has anything to do with it or not. My researches among everyday women have failed to unearth any who can truthfully be said to have this psychological scar. In fact there was one woman of my acquaintance who told me of her young days. She was brought up with four brothers and, as she said, "It was pricks, pricks, at every turn. So much so that when I went to the john I used to try to emulate them, never with any great success." If one listens to the psychiatrists, here is a woman who must by now be in terrible shape. She is one of the most sensible, well-adjusted women I know.

I think the truth of the matter is this: Women themselves hold a low opinion of their pelvic area. As pointed out elsewhere in this book, it is the focal point of constant concern for them—the dread of malodor coming from there, the regular distasteful reminder of menstruation, etc., etc. Themselves so self-conscious about it, they transfer this to a belief that others regard it with distaste ("How could a man ever want to kiss me there?"). It is not so much that they suffer from penis envy but that they are consumed with pelvic self-criticism.

It should be brought home to them that far from their having penis envy it would be much more logical for the male to have clitoris envy.

During the exploratory years of youth boys and girls "play doctor" as an ingenious excuse for intimate reconnoitre, when "let me feel your pulse" has nothing to do with holding the wrist. No doubt is left in the minds of the participants that the main focal point of a high pulse rate is the penis and the clitoris.

It is at this stage, we are given to understand, that girls develop penis envy. But if you look at the thing quite objectively, although the penis is far more showy the clitoris is a much more erogenous affair. And here is an aspect of it that not everybody realizes: In the human body, male or female, the clitoris is the only organ that is there solely for the reason of sex. The breasts, for example, are a source of sexual excitement but they share this with their function of providing milk for the young. The penis is not only a sexual organ; it also has its mundane function. And so on.

But the clitoris, or "the man in the canoe" as it has been termed, exists purely and simply to excite at a touch. It is more highly endowed with nerves than the penis and is therefore much more easily stimulated, the reason for this being the very fact of its single purpose.

If the penis were as highly charged as the clitoris the male would be forever being sexually enlivened whenever bringing the penis into use for its other duty; even hour-by-hour contact with his thighs and clothing would have him perpetually in a fine old state. That is why, in the structure of the female body the ultra-sensitive clitoris is not large and protuberant. So tucked away is it that even its possessor may be getting to be quite a big girl before she learns that she has it, and that knowledge may come to her quite by accident. There is a basic reason why boys, being cowboy-conscious, should far outnumber girls among the clients of riding stables and yet the opposite is the case.

But by whatever way the girl learns of its presence she differs radically from men in that she has there a part of her anatomy geared exclusively to sex, be she in time a housewife, prostitute, nun, fashion model, schoolma'am, maiden aunt, or blue-movie starlet. How large it looms in her life is quite up to the inclinations of the female concerned—"the clitoris only attains its full development and dimensions with regular and constant sexual intercourse, but even in virgins it can become enlarged and active if they themselves are in the habit of applying local friction" (Van de Velde). A doctor in a London hospital has told of his most disturbing experience —being called to Out Patients' Casualty to come to the aid of a nun to dislodge a crucifix that had become embedded.

However, viewing the clitoris as something less embattled than that, there is no question that it should be a source of envy by the male, rather than women being envious of the penis. For one thing it is far more long-wearing.

Impotency is something which can be a great worry to men. And not only older men, who are traditionally the ones upon whom the problem weighs most heavily. I remember a young friend I had in my boardinghouse days in New York. We were all young people in this particular place and included was one good-looking girl who particularly appealed to my friend. The attraction was mutual and one night it was decided that he should share her divan. One little problem, however, was that he was on a different floor from hers and the late night journey entailed his negotiating the stairs and passing the landlady's bedroom before he could achieve his rendezvous. The stairs creaked, the floorboards of the hallway creaked. This was a known fact during daylight hours; how much more so at dead of night when all was quiet in the house.

He did manage the journey, although it took him a considerable time since he had to pause virtually after every step to listen and make sure he hadn't aroused the landlady. Once in the young lady's boudoir, however, all was well. Or rather, he thought all would be well. As it turned out, the eagerly-awaited tryst was a fiasco. He was quite unable to function. Back in his own room, this worried him terribly. Impotent at twenty-two! This was a shattering thought.

In time, of course, he was to realize that he was not impotent at all. It was all psychological. His mind had not been fully on the matter. He had been so fearful all the time that the landlady would burst in and catch them *in flagrante delicto*, he was not concentrating sufficiently. However, it happened his failure so disturbed him that next day he went to a place he knew aids to virility could be obtained and bought some which, on the basis of what was claimed for them, he concluded must surely be the best. And so concerned was he about what he thought was his condition that he took considerably more than the specified dose. The result was more than he bargained for. He had an erection for three weeks. It was most embarrassing. Never without it. He had to take it to the office.

No such problems confront the female and her clitoris. And there is another, even stronger reason why men should have cause for envy. The clitoris is far more sexually satisfactory in that it is a repeater, whereas the penis is a single-shot weapon. Granted that at times of high virility and inaccurate boasting the penis can go through its erectile and ejaculation cycle on several occasions in a relatively short space of time the general thing is that once orgasm has been achieved by the male, interest and everything else flags.

It is not news to say that this pattern does not apply also to women. For them, "The same again, please," right after orgasm is as common as, "I'll have another cup," to the inveterate coffee drinker. This repeater aspect of the clitoris holds good whether in love play, actual intercourse, or during solo endeavor, and what may come as news to some men is the proportions it assumes.

The authoress of *The Sensuous Woman* suggests that any reader who wants to be one should experiment with masturbation workouts to ascertain what her "multiple orgasm pattern" is, in other words—how many can be achieved in a single session. Those who are usually satisfied with three or four should try for ten or twenty-five. Some women are known to reach a hundred before tiredness eventually forces them to call a halt.

A hundred times at one sitting! That is surely something calculated to induce clitoris envy in men. But in fact it doesn't. As has so rightly been said, masturbation is the thief of time, and men have so many other things to get on with.

WHAT APPEALS
(AND DOESN'T APPEAL) TO MEN

Although it is of prime importance for a woman to appeal to the opposite sex (a mate must be won *and* held), women seem to have little conception of what appeals to men. They give every indication of not having studied the subject. They have done no market research.

If they made themselves more aware, then they would not indulge to the great extent they do in the unliked aspects which we shall go into in a moment.

At the risk of stating the obvious, the great appeal that a woman can have for a man is to be feminine, *i.e.*, the antithesis of those female impersonators—Australian girls. But it is surprising the ignorance, even among sophisticated women, of how to make the most of that femininity.

We have seen, in the section of the False Front, how so many females in their attempt to present the ultra-feminine image go for such things as bleached hair, false eyelashes, long fingernails, molded bras and girdles, which achieve the effect of their being hard, stiff, and scratchy, instead of accentuating what a real woman should be—soft and pliant.

For years they have, in great numbers, worn slacks and at time of writing the pants suit is being given another whirl. Why dress like men? Granted, slacks are "practical." But why single out this one sphere in which to be practical, when almost everything about women's garb and makeup is devoted to being impractical? Women's shoes distort their toes . . . false eyelashes make their eyes flick all the time . . . daubing on and scraping off skin lotions ruins the skin . . . for a woman the most wonderful thing about a girdle is taking it off . . . etc., etc. It is completely illogical, isn't it, to devote all that time, effort, and self-torture to having feminine appeal—and then put on slacks, than which there is nothing less feminine. The excuse for wearing the trouser suit is not that it is practical. It is purely and simply going along with what, at this moment, is fashionable. Men pray for the early arrival of the time when it goes out of vogue. The heavy, tweedy material in which it so often comes makes it more appropriate for a man going hunting. Bring back the lace, the frills, the silks, and satins. Look feminine.

I remember being out with a woman who was very well-groomed, as befitted her important job with a cosmetic firm. Sitting down, the lace of her slip showed at the hemline of her dress and she became concerned about this, making adjustments to ensure that it was out of sight.

"Why do you do that?" I asked her. "It is most intriguing, that glimpse of lace."

"Is it really?" she said, naively for a woman who was known to pride herself on attracting and making conquests with males. "Does that appeal to men?"

"Of course it does."

Lace is essentially feminine. By association it bespeaks in men's minds intimacy—feminine undergarments, nightdresses. I was surprised that this woman did not know this basic fact: when a woman lets her slip show when she is standing up it is inefficient; when she lets it show when she is sitting down it is intriguing.

We have dealt earlier with that other good thing—perfume —but in regard to not only what they wear but also what they say and do, herewith . . .

FEMININITIES WHICH DON'T APPEAL TO MEN
And About Which Women Would Be Smart to Do Something

The Big Hat

I call this section The Big Hat to cover a multitude of sins in this regard, of which the wearing of a spectacular, unmanageable hat is the most blatant. You know the sort of thing. She has decided that the weather is fine enough for the outdoor function to enable her to launch her super new milliner's creation which will have all the other women green with envy at how terrific she looks. But as well as the weather being fine, it is windy. The whole damned afternoon she spends making sudden clutches at her hat as each gust of wind whizzes by and sitting there with her hand clamped down on the crown of it when the wind has a sustained blow. You haven't her full attention. In fact you really haven't any of her attention, since controlling that wide-brimmed straw lid of hers is a full-time job. And this was the afternoon you really thought you were going to make some progress with her. . . .

Any women's apparel that comes into the spectacular category is an irritation to a man. He gives an inward groan when he collects a girl to go out and see that she has donned some dress or pants suit that has Trouble written all over it—some festooned concoction of flounces, flares, and ruching that obviously hasn't been properly engineered by the designer because already she's furtively tucking in something that shouldn't be sticking out. A man naturally likes the girl he takes out to look attractive, because it flatters his ego ("Look what *I've* got!"), but he would much prefer her to be an eye-catcher by the very simplicity and good taste of what she is wearing. A girl who is in something unostentatious which is beautifully tailored and with just the right accessories can give her escort her full attention because she knows in the back of her mind that she has achieved what she set out to do—get envious looks from other women and appreciative glances from the men. Something I once saw above the entrance to a university put it in a nutshell: "Simplicity and Unity are the True Keynotes of Beauty."

In this field is that other source of embarrassment to men —the girl who is not normally a sex bomb but suddenly decides to be BOLD. She gets herself a dress with a low-cut neckline that is such a slash that she knows it will have men's eyes popping. And then what happens? Throughout the even-

ing she spends her time fingering the lower part of the revealing V, holding it together a couple of inches up, while the
man she is with feels like saying in exasperation: "If you've
decided to let them show, *let* them show."

House Proudery

I recall once dropping in on an acquaintance and being surprised to see him sitting in an armchair in his living room
holding a blown-up paper bag. At first I thought he was going
to bang it against his other hand and produce a minor explo-
sion to amuse his youngsters. But that wasn't at all the function of the blown-up paper bag.

He was smoking a cigar and confessed to me shamefacedly
that his wife said that cigar smoke got into the drapes and
made them smell—so he had to exhale into the bag. Clearly
here was a man henpecked beyond recall. This was house
proudery carried to the ultimate.

Such excesses are, I hope, not common, but there are few
males, from boyhood to their mature years, who have not
suffered at the hands of the house-proud female. When she
screams, "Don't walk on that floor, I've just washed it!" it is
no good trying to be jocular about the thing and saying,
"Who are you expecting—the President?" That only makes
things worse. You let yourself in for, "How can I be expected
to have the place looking nice if . . ."

Thick and fast come the clichés of house proudery:
"What a mess!" . . . "I've just had those slipcovers done" . . .
"Pick that up!" . . . "Don't put that down there!" . . . "There
are such things as ashtrays, you know" . . . "If you like living
in a pigsty, I don't!" . . . etc., etc.

Men pray for the day when women will realize that a
house does not exist to be kept clean, period. It is there to be
kept clean to be lived in.

One Excuse Is Enough

Although he used it for evil ends, Goebbels had an axiom

which was very sound: "If you are going to lie, it is much more effective to tell one big lie than a lot of little ones."

This could not be more applicable than in the matter of making excuses. Women have never learned that when wanting to get out of doing something they don't want to do, one excuse is convincing but using more than one excuse is a dead giveaway.

For example, a man in whom a girl is not interested phones to invite her out and she says, "Oh, what a pity, I've just washed my hair." True or false, that gets rid of him, in one blow. But if instead she says, "I don't think I really feel up to going out tonight, and besides, my mother said something about dropping over for a while. . . ." That fatal "and besides" is a sure indication to him that what comes after it is a succession of excuses for getting out from under the invitation. She then will find herself involved in a long, tedious exchange of dialogue as he tries to demolish each excuse.

The same thing applies to a wife on the phone. She has answered it, to learn that it is the Wilkinsons with an invitation to dinner on Friday. The boring Wilkinsons are the last people you want to have dinner with. If the husband had answered the phone he would have made it short, sharp, and effective by saying something unassailable like, "I'm off to Boston tomorrow," foolproof because even if you bump into the Wilkinsons on the appointed day his office changed the dates of his Boston trip. But with his wife on the phone the poor husband squirms as he listens to her performance: "Friday . . . I *think* our baby-sitter has her Spanish dancing lessons on Fridays . . . I can check . . . but as a matter of fact *this* Friday isn't a good day for us, now that I come to think of it, because my husband has a business friend of his coming to town to see the big game on Saturday and I don't know whether we'll have to entertain him on the Friday . . ."

And so on and *on*, until her man echoes the heartfelt plea of husbands throughout the world: "For God's sake, woman, think up one good excuse and stick to it."

Inability to Hold Their Liquor

There is nothing quite so unattractive to see and as tedious to cope with as a woman drunk.

It would all be much simpler if women drank beer. A survey of drinking habits conducted by the market research department of United Glass revealed that of the men asked, seventy-nine percent said they drank beer in bars and only thirty-eight percent of the women did. In other words four out of five men and only two out of five women drank beer. The survey, concerned only with the containers they used for drinking, did not go into the matter of quantity but one knows from observation that the two out of five women do not quaff beer the way the four men do. Brewers, though lacking the statistics to back it up, will tell you that women drink very little beer.

Why? In the first place they don't particularly like the taste of beer. And second, "they are smaller biologically and need less liquor in bulk to top up their batteries," as one brewer put it to me. This latter is an interesting point and a complete reversal of the generally held view that women have a larger capacity, as evidenced by their being able to hold out longer before having to pay a visit to the rest room. The simple fact is that not being great downers of the brew, their fluid intake is much less.

The result of their disinterest in beer is of course that they get involved with booze, they drink the hard stuff. This has a financial aspect which acts against them. Many girls miss out on a great deal of fun and are left out in the cold by prospective male companions, young men who can manage it on beer but can just not afford to finance evenings out with a girl who is on gin, or whiskey or, worse still, the type who responds to your query of what will you have with, "Oh, anything," and then names some outlandishly expensive concoction. And the poor fellow has to sit there when he is in need of a refill, doing a mental check on his immediate finances to see whether he has enough to sponsor another.

But apart from the dampening effect it has on young-love-on-a-shoestring, the female necessity to drink liquor can be a frequent cause of embarrassment and annoyance to men. It stands to reason that the hard liquor drinker is going to get drunk more quickly than the beer drinker. And worse than getting drunk is being ill, for which many women have a proclivity. One reason for this is that they will embark on the most complicated type of drinks from bottles that men would never ask of a barman. Then, shipped home by embarrassed husband or boyfriend, between visits to the john they try to sell the story that, "Those shrimps we had for dinner must have been off."

Even when they do have sufficient sense to stick to the less exotic whiskey or gin-and-tonic they are not sensible enough to drink properly. Intelligent males "pace" their drinking, i.e., if they feel they are getting under the weather they will have a sandwich or some other form of blotting paper because they know there is the rest of the evening untouched and they don't want to flake out when things might be at their most interesting. Women do not pace their drinking in this way.

When a woman starts to feel a glow she is likely to have another drink on the supposition that it will give her even more of a glow. Fair enough. But when she has yet another, her man sees the danger signs. "Let's have something to eat," he says. "Oh, no," she says. "I don't want any food. It would only take the edge off. I feel marvelous! I'll have another!" And off she embarks on trying to multiply one glow by a third, fourth, and fifth drink, never learning that when you feel good you can't feel five times as good, you merely get unutterably sloshed.

Liquor being the great ridder of inhibitions, many men, without needing Dorothy Parker to inform them that "candy is dandy but liquor is quicker," have long been using alcoholic beverages as a means of furthering their sexual interest in the aloof female. But the experienced philanderer will tell you that this is something which has to be gauged to a nicety.

There are pitfalls, not the least of which is the situation when, his fiendish scheme having reached that point when the Big Moment has arrived, instead of, "Oh my God, Cecil, take me!" what does he hear? "I think I'm going to be sick."

The link between drinking and women being ill is one of long standing and something which, unfortunately, men constantly have to chide women about.

My wife tells the story against herself of the time she was leaving the old home town to go up to the big city to further her career in journalism. The boss of the paper she was leaving and some of his cronies saw her off on the train. In the course of the farewell drinks in her compartment he said that, being a woman, she would not be able to stay the course of newspaper drinking in New York. She had no option but to take up the challenge when the shots of rum he poured became more and more generous. It was a tough assignment and she kept furtively checking her watch to see whether she would be able to last to train time. The final send-off drink was such a stiff one that she felt that if she was going to beat off their challenge on behalf of womanhood, she would have to water it down before she could drink it. Luckily there was a diversion out on the platform and when they looked out to see what it was she craftily slipped the drink behind her back and pressed the button at the washstand. "Toss it off!" the men said as train time came and this had to be the last drink. Down it went. They gave her a little round of applause, gaily trooped off, and left her on her way to the big city. Thereupon she was violently ill. But it must be stated in her defense that the men had not all succeeded in proving that women can't hold their liquor. When she had pulled her little trick of watering down her drink she had pressed the wrong button and had diluted it with liquid soap.

A Glimpse Into the Unknown

The definition of a shaggy-dog story as being "like seeing a girl get out of a sports car—either you see it at once or you never see it" brings into sharp focus a divergence of male and female opinion. It is doubtful whether it will ever be resolved.

Alan Brien, the English newspaper columnist who endeared himself to me ever since I read his comment that "words are alcohol to the Irish but the trouble is, so is alcohol," not long ago dealt with this subject adroitly. He wrote:

The incongruity between what women hide and men seek is epitomized by the controversy over the famous Gap, now (unhappily) almost obliterated by new styles of underwear. Few women can understand that a glimpse of bare flesh between the stocking top and the garter belt has sustained many of us through long sessions in the front row of political meetings, enlivened slow journeys on the subway escalator and made it a pleasure to close car doors for strange females. To them it seems a sloppy, inefficient revelation of backstage machinery, the strings of the marionette, scaffolding which should not be on show. To us, schoolboy *voyeurs* that we remain, it is an insight into work in progress, a squint into the Green Room, a confirmation that everything has not been bought in a shop.

This has all been going on for a very long time. In the Victorian era it was the excitement of the glimpse of an ankle. For a period during the eighteenth century when women wore voluminous skirts with nothing on underneath, men were at pains to congregate in areas where they went riding, in the ardent hope that they would see them falling off horses. With the shorter skirts of more modern times there is not the need of such complicated planning, but still it is the continuing story of women trying to hide what men seek to see.

It should be noted that the advent of pantyhose, tights, call them what you will, has not outdated this situation. For one thing, pantyhose has not completely replaced the conventional garter belt and stockings. It has merely meant that the latter are now less frequently seen. Which has had the effect of heightening the whole thing. They have taken on some of the trappings of a collector's item.

And also there is this other point. When a woman really wants to look her best—when all dressed up for an Occasion —she will invariably opt for the good old-fashioned garter belt and stockings, since they are far more efficient for the well-groomed leg look. And the very fact that she is doing her utmost to look *soignée* makes a glimpse of what Alan Brien calls the "backstage machinery" all the more intriguing to a man.

A woman checking her undercarriage when she sits down is a trained reflex dating right back to when she was a little girl and used to sit on the steps of the front porch, legs apart, panties fully on view, and her mother had to tell her that nice little girls didn't sit like that. Now it is automatic when seating herself, the checking of the position of the skirt to ensure that nobody can see up there, even to a prim tucking in at the sides, to make sure that there isn't a wide-angle view. And during her sojourn on the seat she'll instinctively double-check from time to time, especially if she's in a hotel lobby, say, and that man across from her doesn't seem to be really reading that newspaper he's holding.

But one must not come away with the impression that this is purely and simply related to sex. A woman who is sexually inclined, who is not averse to getting into bed with a man, even the one with the newspaper if the circumstances are right, such a woman will still go through the skirt-tucking-in exercise. It is very misleading. Here is a young woman who to the male viewer seems to exude sex and yet when she sits down she fusses about the position of her skirt like a Sunday school teacher. The thing is, of course, that sex doesn't come into it as far as she is concerned. The overriding consideration is that she wants to look her best and to her, stocking tops are unsightly.

It is interesting that the male and the female attitude toward stocking tops should be so diametrically opposed, that what is unsightly to one is exciting to the other. But the point about it all is this: It is the very fact that women are perpetually trying to stop men seeing their stocking tops that makes it all so exciting. If women were not fastidious about it and they could be seen regularly, without any sense of achievement on the part of the male, he would at once agree with her. Stocking tops *would* look unsightly, as unsightly as hair rollers and straying shoulder straps.

Hoarding a Mad

The basic difference between women and men when they get annoyed oddly parallels their different sexuality. We have seen that in sex it is usual for the male to come to his climax and then that's that; the female, slower of arousal, can taper off gradually after climax or continue at once to further orgasms. It is an altogether much more drawn-out matter with the female.

Precisely the same thing applies to a woman getting mad.

Annoyance in a man is invariably an explosive affair. Irked by something in the home or at the office, he will blow his top. He will give vent to his feelings, verbally or physically, and then, having got his displeasure out of his system, the graph of his annoyance will show a sudden decline. He has made use of his safety valve and then all is over and forgotten.

But this is not the customary female approach. Take the situation where a woman is confronted by a Cause for Annoyance.

Maybe her husband had promised and promised that he would get tickets for Tony Bennett when he came to town, left it until too late and she was the only one in her set who didn't get to see him.

Maybe she passed in front of the TV set just as Green Bay was scoring the winning touchdown and it was not so much her husband telling her to get her fat rump out of the way but the inference that it is a fat rump.

Or at the country club dance when he and that newcomer to the community with cleavage down to her navel were seen to make way out on to the terrace at the same time.

Anyway, she feels she has been WRONGED.

Confronted with a Situation, a woman either (a) blows up right away or (b) hoards her mad, saves it up for an extended period or (c) presents her husband with a combination of the two. Whatever she does, however, you can be certain that it is not a one-time flare-up, not just an explosive letting off of the safety valve, for normal running to be resumed right afterward.

There is a definite routine and predictable dialogue with a woman hoarding a mad and you can be sure that at this very moment somewhere this sort of exchange is taking place:

He: "You're being very quiet, what's wrong?"
She: "Nothing's wrong."
"But you haven't said anything for the last—"
"I just don't feel like talking."
"There's something bugging you. What is it?"
"Nothing's wrong."
"You feel all right?"
"I feel perfectly all right, thank you very much."
And so on and so on.

A woman can prolong this sort of thing indefinitely. Without any trouble at all she can make it last three days, which is a good general average among females.

But of course an astute man knows that it is the easiest thing in the world to break through this "Nothing's Wrong" barrier. All he needs to do is something along these lines: Opening his mail, he reads one of the letters and exclaims, "Ye Gods!"; or returning from talking on the phone he mutters to himself "Amazing, I can't believe it." Any curiosity-arouser like that will suffice. It at once places the women in what, for a female, is an awful predicament. Having embarked on the spinning out of her annoyance, she is now consumed with curiosity—"Has he had a sudden windfall, which'll mean we can have a really good vacation this year?", "Has Bob broken with Alice, which means I'd be the first to be able to tell everybody?" The wise man knows that her curiosity will win hands down over her conspiracy of silence, and the senseless waste of time that that female wile involves will be cut short.

Hoarding a mad, the eager embracing of a mood of anger and the determination to spin it out as long as possible, is a female characteristic that has no counterpart in men, except of course with the homosexual or other effeminate type. In fact it is one of the main yardsticks in gauging effeminacy in men, a prime example of "behaving like a woman." One of the most effective sequences in that superb play and film, *The Odd Couple*, was that in which the two men were "not speaking."

Why do women do it? It is of course purely and simply a maneuver to get attention. While she is employing these aloof, uncommunicative tactics a woman becomes the focal point of her husband (or boyfriend when the unmarried female resorts to it). He wants to have the whole thing out, clear the air, and then he can get on with his other interests. But as long as she has him in a state of, "For Christ's sake, what are you mad about—tell me!", she has him unable to concentrate on other things, thinking only of her.

It takes time, this tiresome stratagem. That's why men, when boys, did it, in the form of sulking. They had the time (the long summer vacation stretching before them—"I've got nothing to do"). But after growing up, their lives becoming fully occupied, they just haven't the time to spare to indulge in it, if indeed they ever have the inclination.

It is a perfect thing for women to liberate themselves from.

The "I'm Paying For This" Tug-of-War

Men never cease to wonder why when women are out together at a restaurant or coffee shop, there's going to be an argument when the check comes:

"It's mine."

"It's *mine. I* invited *you.*"

"But it's my turn." (To waitress: "Don't take her money.")

"Mildred, if you pay for this, I'll never come out with you again."

Etc., etc.

It can develop into physical exchange, with a tussle over possession of the check that can become as heated as two terriers disputing a bone. To forestall such tug-of-wars, some women develop the fine art of what might be called the "Check Snatch" (flicking a hand out to snare it the moment it hits the table). It seems that they devote the whole meal to just waiting for this triumphant moment.

There's never any such argument between men over payment for a meal. The dialogue is invariably restricted to something like this:

"It's about time I bought *you* a lunch."

Silence. (Thinks: "You're damned right it is.")

Why is it a female characteristic to be forever going through this "Put Your Money Away" performance? Any woman who has given the matter some thought will tell you that it is a demonstration of good old empathy—that quality that we girls have in such generous measure and you men lack. Even if financially it is just the price of a couple of coffees, the one woman is giving the other tangible proof of her empathy toward the other: "Let me pay this and it will show how fond of you I am, how much I admire the way you're standing up under the strain of your husband having it off regularly with that hot-panted computer operator at the office."

The Five Most Overworked Feminine Clichés

From the keen competition among the stock remarks which women use over and *over* again, from "I have nothing to wear" to "What will people think?", I choose these five as the most hackneyed:

"It's all very well for you!"—The sort of situation when this is trotted out is that she dropped her shopping getting it out of the car and the brand new set of rollers which she had just bought got saturated in ketchup and her husband isn't interested in hearing about it. The reason for his disinterest is that he is too busy wondering to himself how on earth he is going to raise the $200,000 to meet the bank's note on the fifteenth and save his business from collapse. Wives have a knack of thinking they are the only people in the world with problems—the Martyr Complex.

"Talk to me."—The poor fellow has got home from a terrible day at work. Surrounded by jabber all day, with the tirades from his boss, the arguments with his subordinates, and the chattering of the secretaries still ringing in his ears, he is only too glad to settle down and relax in the quiet of his home. And his wife says: "Talk to me."

"What's happening to us?"—This is straight out of the movies, that one about the marriage that seems to be on the rocks but all comes right in the end. Pure Hollywood, like that other lovely cliché from the hospital film: "There's only one man who can save your child's life, madam, and he's in Vienna." What's happening to us? *Everybody* knows what's happening to us. The high polish of young marriage has worn off and we're now down to the realities of trying to live in harmony together.

"I'm tired."—*He's* tired, too. He's had a tough day at the office and has spent the evening working on figures to present to tomorrow's meeting. Tired, yes . . . but what better way to drift off to sleep than in the arms of his wife? But of course her "I'm tired" doesn't mean "I'm tired." It means: "You can forget about sex tonight, my friend."

"Tell me you love me."—Oh, my God!

The Teaser

The type of female which men undoubtedly dislike most is the teaser. I do not include the professional stripteaser in this category. She earns an honest living by catering to the male craving for visual stimulation. The amateur teaser, *la femme terrible de la chaise longue*, is dishonest not only with her victim but with herself. She undertakes a contract which she knows she is not going to fulfill.

Why do females indulge in this least attractive of their activities?

In youth there is the mitigating factor that the young girl is merely embarking on some practical research to augment the pure theory of her furtive peeks at Mother's medical book on *The Human Body*. The girl, who like as not is not fully clear in her mind as to how one gets stuck with a baby, definitely does not want to run the risk. Also she wants to avoid being branded along with the type of girl (of which there is always at least one to be found in every local community and of which it can be said that she has been tried and found wanton), who lets boys do *anything* and isn't above letting grown men do a bit of delving, for a consideration. So, in the young good girl it can be regarded as forgivable.

But definitely not when she is past the experimental stage.

When she becomes a young woman and still teases there are a variety of reasons for her behavior.   .

There is a whole group, worldwide and reaching its highest concentration in Italy, Spain, Southern Ireland, and the Province of Quebec, for whom the explanation is a religious one. If you've ever been to a nurses' party at an Irish Catholic hospital you will soon realize why things wind up with the young doctors drinking and singing songs around the piano while the beautiful colleens are huddled in a group exchanging hen chat. The men, from experience, just can't be bothered exposing themselves to the prick-teasing that religious dogma imposes on the young females.

But girls not bound by such religious strictures can be equally distasteful in their behavior. More than a few make a career of being teasers. Why? Dismissing dread of disease with a mention, fear of pregnancy is the basic. And the advent of the Permissive Society and the Pill has not as yet fundamentally changed what goes on in darkened living rooms across the country.

The "Let's wait until we're married" type of teaser may be pardoned for her admirable effort to retain the Old Values. But there are two types which are absolutely despicable.

The first is the sort of girl who wears low-cut necklines, thrust-out sweaters, gives mini-skirted leg displays, shrinks her jeans to ensure an adhesive-plaster fit to crotch and buttocks, in all ways projects the Sex Bomb image and then when a male not unnaturally makes a pass at her turns indignantly on him: "What sort of a girl do you think I am!"

When asked why she regales herself so provocatively, she can only answer petulantly: "Why shouldn't I?"

This is a type of sexual dishonesty which is exclusively feminine, of which there is no male equivalent whatsoever.

And the other is the mature woman who indulges in calculated teasing, who employs the Puppet-on-a-String technique. She hasn't got youth on her side any more, she spends a great deal of time before the dressing table mirror with her chin jutting up in the air running her fingers up and down on her extended throat checking again and again for those telltale lines. There's a man interested in her. How best to hold on to him? If she consents to get into bed with him it could be all over and done with afterward. Better to keep him on the end of a string by calling a halt each time. He'll be annoyed on each occasion, go away mad. But he'll be back. Want to bet?

The type of teaser who is to be pitied rather than despised is the suburban housewife who yearns for Involvement and then, when it comes along, is scared to go along with it.

Over and over again the pattern is repeated of the housewife who has got the kids off to school. She's having a cup of coffee before doing the breakfast dishes. A tune on the radio, the mellow spring sunshine starting the sap rising, or happening to brush her arm against her breasts as she reaches for the sugar, *something* sets her mind off on a sexual tangent. She runs her hand down over her stomach and thrusts up against her stressed palm. "Oh, my God," she says. And then realizes that five to ten in the morning with the dishes in the sink and the beds to be made is no time to be getting aroused. She puts from her mind whichever male movie star happens to be No. 1 on her fantasy parade that month and sets about her chores.

But she can't help thinking to herself that life is dull, dull, dull. If only she could become involved with an attractive, interesting man who would bring a heartwarming change of pace to her humdrum existence. . . .

The answer to this particular type of If Only is often close at hand. The frustrated suburban housewife's delight—the Man Who Works at Home. He may be a commercial artist, writer, TV actor, antique picture-frame restorer. Anyway, he's around most days, when the conventional husbands are at the office.

One such who has newly moved into the neighborhood could have observed our housewife for a while and decided that the time has come for: "I wonder whether I could borrow your clippers? My hedge is in terrible shape." She is responsive: "While you're here would you like some coffee? Or a drink? Or is it too early in the day for a drink?" (Nervous laugh.)

Involvement is under way. And you can be pretty certain that with it comes the teasing.

The barriers put up by our housewife when the chips are down take countless forms:

How can she bring herself to it in this house paid for by her hard-working husband? . . . Young Johnnie's baseball bat and glove over there in the corner are a reproof . . . What would Tricia think of her mother if she could see her at this moment halfway out of her blouse with Mr. Wilkie from the house on the corner?

So, what we get is this sort of thing:

"We can't! My mother/sister/next door neighbor has a habit of dropping in unexpectedly."

"I'm very fond of your wife. I'd hate to do anything to hurt her."

"No! No! If I let you do that, I can't answer for what I'd do. I'm not made of ice, you know."

"If only we could get away for a while, just you and I together. It would be quite different then. You'd see."

But they never do. And he doesn't.

It is all very sad. Enshrouding domesticity turns her into a prick-teaser, something she dislikes herself for being as much as it annoys him.

On its everyday level teasing produces in men frustrated annoyance leading to arguments, recriminations, and eventual contempt. But it can go beyond that and if one would read about the sort of repercussions it can have one should read the short story, "Virtue," by Somerset Maugham. Although it is not as well known as "Rain" and some of his others, I would regard it among his best.

It concerns a young man on extended leave in London from the rubber plantations of Malaya. He meets a not unattractive married woman and would like nothing better than to get into bed with her after his long stretch of limited opportunity overseas. But she will have none of it. She accepts his invitations to dinner, the theater, and the other attentions he pays her but draws the line at anything more than a chaste embrace. The more she denies him the more preoccupied he becomes with his desire to make love to her. Since she is no longer young and has settled into the rut of a dreary marriage, having this young man infatuated with her, as she regards it, is a great boost to her self-esteem. What to the man is merely a persistent effort to break through her teasing and get her into bed is in her mind a Great Love.

Complications develop and result in her husband's suicide. As Maugham points out, the whole thing becomes a disaster which could all have been obviated if the silly woman had merely had a wholesome roll in the hay with the young planter. In a very simple way this would have both satisfied his needs after a long lay-off and restored her feeling that she still has appeal for men.

That, of course, was fiction. But such things can happen in real life. . . .

Some years ago in London a man I knew fairly well was entertaining a couple from abroad, from the country where he had formerly lived and he invited me to dinner to meet them. He was a big, tanned, taciturn man who owned a vast, very lucrative cattle ranch back home. She was a very good-looking young woman, vivacious, well-groomed and expensively dressed, as befitted the fact that they had made a suite at Claridge's their headquarters during their holiday in England.

At that time I happened to be writing a novel which had a woman as its central character and I was interested in what life would be like for this particular woman living miles from anywhere with only men around her. She was very open.

"I stand at the window of my bedroom," she said, "and watch them bringing the cattle in. They're stripped to the waist in the heat and the dust gathers on their skin like the fuzz on peaches. I like to see them crack those long whips they have. They have no handles, you know. They're plaited all the way down to the part that you hold, which is thicker than the rest of the whip."

There was an uneasy pause. Her husband seemed displeased. I changed the subject.

During the meal she flirted with my friend and when her husband was unhappy about this she laughed and said not to worry, they had known each other for years. Shortly afterward I learned that when her husband took the three of them to a fashionable nightclub, my friend had been dancing with

her and when they returned to the table the husband an-
nounced very firmly that they were going. He paid the waiter
for the full, barely-begun meal and for all the wine they had
ordered. The waste of money did not matter to him financially but when I heard about it it struck me that he was getting
unnecessarily worked up about the Other Man. After all, one
could feel sure that she would not be unwise enough to give
up all the security and the good things of life she enjoyed in
favor of my friend, who quite frankly led a rather precarious
life.

Not long after the couple returned home he moved away
from my district and we were out of touch for some time.
When we did meet again we were reminiscing and I said:

"What ever happened to that woman who came over to
London who used to be an old flame of yours?"

"Janet? Oh, she's living in the South of France now. Loads
of money."

"Her husband retired?"

"No. He didn't retire. He's dead. He committed suicide."

"Good grief."

"He made one of those senseless gestures. He was driven
out of his mind with jealousy. He blew his brains out with a
shotgun, outside the door of her bedroom. It was a ghastly
business. She heard the shot in the middle of the night and
got up to see what it was, and opened the door of her
room . . ."

In a moment he added thoughtfully, "She's an odd one,
that Janet."

"Why do you say that?"

"I've known her for years. Grew up with her. We were
smitten with each other for a while. But I never had any sex
with her. I don't know of any man who did."

12 THE "HOW AM I DOING?" COMPLEX

We all receive letters from women—a girl friend, wife, mother, sister, mistress—and you may or may not have noticed that there is an interesting little thing about letters from women, a way in which they differ from men's letters. Women are forever apologizing for the quality of their handwriting—"please pardon this scrawl," followed by an excuse which can range from, "I am writing this in bed," through "I'm rushing to catch the mail," to "I really must get a new pen."

Men rarely, if ever, make mention of their handwriting in a letter. They are concerned solely with the information they are conveying, not with what the recipient will think of the penmanship.

This is a small matter but it reflects the whole basic difference in the makeup of men and women. Men are objective; women subjective. Women worry constantly about what sort of impression they are making—the "How am I doing?" complex.

There is an interesting little test you can make next time you are at a bar on a quiet night when people are killing time bringing out their favorite party tricks. Tell some man you will give him a test to see whether he has feminine tendencies and then ask him to do these three things: (a) strike a match, (b) look at his fingernails, and (c) take a drink from his glass.

If he is all-male he will strike the match away from himself (women strike matches toward themselves, not having the good sense to bear in mind that the head of the match may fly into the face); he will look at his fingernails bunched in the palm of his hand (women extend the hand with fingernails spread out fanlike, looking at the fingernails from the back of the hand, a habit they have from not wanting to smear newly applied nail polish); and he will look down into his glass as he drinks.

The last item is the one that concerns us here. Observe most women when they are at a party, say, or out for dinner at a fashionable restaurant and you will see that they cannot rest from looking about to see what sort of impression they are making, even when they are taking a drink. A woman with a glass to her lips will not be looking down into the glass as a man does, but over the rim of it, with that how-am-I-doing look.

This subjectivity (or in the dictionary definition "reference to one's self, or ego, rather than to one's environment") permeates the whole feminine being. It is most rampant in the home, not unnaturally, since that is where women are most.

For example, husbands have learned that they dare not make any criticism, however mild, of any dish that their wives put before them. If they are unwise enough to pass a casual comment such as "This meat's a bit tough," they leave themselves open to an outburst: "It's all very well for you, you don't have to run a house and look after three kids and do all the shopping and the laundry, etc., etc. . . ." until at length, hidden away at the end, is the information that she was so busy that day that she didn't have time to select a really good roast. Women's lack of objectivity is such that any comment on the food a man eats in his home is regarded by her as a personal affront—a vicious attack upon her capabilities as wife, mother, and homemaker. Even the oblique approach such as that used by the more kindly theater and other critics—"This is not up to your usual high standard"— will not absolve a husband from a tirade which can, on occasion, be prolonged over several days.

A friend of mine was once confronted with a dish called "Shrimp Creole" which his wife had read about in some women's magazine. Not only did he not have any great liking for shrimp but also the concoction, in his wife's hands, was a disaster. But he was discreet enough to eat it and say nothing. This apparently was taken by his wife for approval. The result is that he has been served "Shrimp Creole" every month or so for the past four years and has still not been able to pluck up the courage to tell his wife he can't abide it. The only winner in this transaction is the cat, which is pleasantly surprised to get a nice big dollop of "Shrimp Creole" if the man's wife is called to the telephone. My friend now prays for phone calls for his wife on "Shrimp Creole" nights.

This subjectivity women take with them when they go out to work and the fact that any comment on anything with which they are directly associated is taken as a personal attack makes them extremely difficult to deal with.

My own office experience with women consisted mainly in dealings with them as staff writers when I was an editor.

When I had cause to have a male writer in about a story he had written there would be discussion, perhaps argument, about the various points I felt didn't come up to scratch, and then he would say, "Okay, I'll do it again," and go off and rewrite it according to the wishes of the editor, who presumably was paid to know how things should be written for the paper.

But with a woman writer . . . No matter how carefully the words of criticism are chosen, one can see the lump forming in the throat, the tears held back and then when it is all over the dash to the powder room and the hankie thrust to the face with the other hand—and once in the feminine security of the powder room, the tear-drenched lamentation: "He hates me!"

Without risking a similar performance one cannot even suggest to a secretary that the filing cabinets could do with a bit of straightening because a letter from International Instruments Inc. is difficult to find when filed under W.

Women in offices are quite incapable of looking objective-

ly upon the thing under discussion and of understanding that
the object of the operation is to have it done as effectively
and efficiently as possible. Their subjectivity invites them to
believe that criticism by a boss is not a self-contained thing,
concerned merely with the matter at hand. To them it goes
much deeper. It is an indication that he doesn't like *me* any
more.

Some women can be objective (prostitutes, for instance)
but the general female inability to stand off from a thing and
regard it impersonally is something that influences so many
aspects of their lives.

It is the reason, for example, why the average woman will
go into a dither in a crisis and the man will keep his head and
try to figure out how best to cope with the situation. Men
will even willingly expose themselves to other people's crises.
Who ever heard of a woman's fire brigade? Women take pre-
cedence over everybody else when the ship's sinking and it's a
case of "Women and children first!" Despite their much
vaunted superiority over men at intricate work, when do you
ever see a woman bomb defuser?

Their innate characteristic of personalizing things makes
them unreliable and inadequate in innumerable spheres. It
stops them, for instance, from appearing side-by-side with
men among the great surgeons. To the male surgeon it is a
matter of what best to do for this young girl who unfortunately must come under the knife: to the woman faced with
the same thing it is: "Oh, my God, if this were my Trudy
who had to have this operation!"

It stops them from being major poets. Remember? If one
looks up the word *subjectivity* in the *Winston Dictionary*,
which was being published in Philadelphia not too long ago,
one sees that only one example of its application is quoted:
"The subjectivity of Mrs. Browning as shown in her sonnets."

One wonders how on earth the feminists hope to deal with
this problem of women's subjectivity, apart from ignoring it,
which seems to be all they've done so far. How can Women's

Lib demand that women must be allowed to do this or that when by their very nature they lack the unflappable objectivity that so many jobs demand? Would *you* want a woman on the floor of the Stock Exchange handling your money when there's a run on the market?

I3   DOING WHAT COMES NATIONALLY

It is always said that you cannot generalize about people. I disagree. Just take this as an example. When a new company is being launched it is customary to print at the top of letters sent out to prospective investors an impressive list of office-holders calculated to inspire confidence that the new firm is a reputable, sound investment. Would you pack such a list with the names of used car dealers?

You certainly can make valid generalizations about certain groups of people, nationalities, and so on. Therefore I have no hesitation at all in generalizing about the women of various nations.

Irish Girls

Irish colleens are beautiful things. But they *are* tiresome. They are the direct cause of young Irishmen being the way they are. Irish girls have a religious problem which cuts right across their fulfilling themselves as women until they are well and truly married.

As one Irishman put it to me: "All right, so we get drunk and we sing and we argue and we fight. We Irishmen are out on our own; we are thrown together as men because our girls are a bunch of teasers and we can't be bothered with them. Having done our drinking and singing and fighting, we then decide it's time to get married and settle down, and we pick one of them out and we breed with her. That is the Irish formula."

Australian Girls

These are great. They are wonderful at being "one of the boys." They can down their beer with the best of men. They wear their hair short—just the thing for swimming at Bondi, Coogee, and Manly Beach. On the yacht they can pee over the side, always to leeward of course, just like men. That's the whole trouble. They are just like men. They are about as feminine as a jockstrap.

The Frenchwoman

Frenchwomen are the real professionals at being women, in the best possible sense.

With less money to spend on clothes than, for example, the women of America (which is a more prosperous country) or of England (where dress materials, woolens and ready-to-wear garments are far less expensive), Frenchwomen contrive to bring flair to whatever they wear—that little touch which sets off a simple outfit and which results, when she is abroad, in heads turned in her direction and the comment: "I bet she's French."

It is paralleled by the artistry she brings, for the same reason, to the preparation of food. Lacking an abundance of meat and other viands, she must make what she has inviting by the judicious use of wine in cooking and by thinking up piquant sauces.

She works at those things to get them right and she has similarly devoted much thought and effort to something else which in her wisdom she feels is important—pleasing men. In her handling of men she is the true expert, the ultimate artist in femininity.

Scandinavian Girls

The attractive Scandinavian girl, of which there are a great number, is long-legged, finely proportioned, her blonde hair is the ideal at which those who bleach aim but are never quite able to achieve, her smooth creamy skin tans to an appealing honey shade. They are the Golden Girls. They have impact. Entrance of a Scandinavian beauty at a party can be guaranteed to stop conversation dead.

But having said all that, one must confess that the Scandinavian girl has a national characteristic of not being very bright. Time and again one has the experience of taking one out for the evening, or having a more intimate relationship, for they are noted for their sexual generosity, only to find that verbally they are pretty heavy going. It is not a matter of the language barrier. The simple truth is that, summing up Scandinavian girls in comparison with others, rarely does one encounter such an abundance of beauty allied to such a paucity of brains.

Greek Interlude

This is all I know about Greek girls.

In my youth I got involved in the Greek Civil War, which ran concurrently with World War II; the British and others of the Allied Forces supported the established government against the EAM insurgents. We were holed up in the middle of Athens, entirely surrounded by the EAM in our headquarters at the Grande Bretagne Hotel. (We lived by candlelight when the EAM blew up the main power plant, and by lighted bootlaces immersed in wax when the candles ran out.) From buildings overlooking downtown Athens the long-range snipers of the EAM fired at anyone in Allied uniform who moved on the streets, which among other things gives me my very own Churchill anecdote—a Churchill story to which I feel I have patent rights, since I was standing beside him when he made the comment. With a typical Churchillian gesture he had come out from England, in person, to solve the Greek Civil War problem. To show the flag he decided to wear the uniform of his honorary rank of Air Vice-Marshal of the RAF, despite the fact that people tried to dissuade him in view of the snipers' special interest in anyone in uniform, particularly British. On top of that, he slipped his security guards, in order to have a stroll around the town to see what was up. But he hadn't gone more than a hundred yards or so when a bullet whizzed past his head and ricocheted from the wall behind him. He looked in the direction from which the sniper's shot had come and said: "What infernal cheek."

Thus having set the scene, let's get to the girls.

The Allied troops in Greece had been brought over from Southern Italy. It had been tough for them there. Not only was it a thankless task slogging up the mountains against an enemy entrenched in high ground, but also when out of the line the opportunities for relaxation were not good. Southern Italy is one of the most rigidly Roman Catholic areas in the world. There were only two types of female relaxation for the troops—good girls and prostitutes, none of what has been termed "enthusiastic amateurs." It was a choice. Either you were invited into the home of a good girl (and all that happened was that you sat around talking to her and her family in the parlor while the spaghetti settled) or you went to a brothel, which wasn't of very great appeal (on the wall outside one of them a soldier had chalked: "Come early and avoid the rash").

In complete contrast were the girls in Greece, directly traceable to the fact that it is of a different religion—Greek Orthodox. Not held in check by the strictures of Roman Catholicism, the Greek girls approached any male-female association with a zest that was a stimulating change from what the troops had encountered across the water in the south of Italy.

But there was a problem. The friendly young ladies of Athens society lived in the better residential districts and these were on the other side of the EAM perimeter. It was quite impossible for any of the beleaguered Allied officers in the Grande Bretagne Hotel to say to a girl: "I'll come and pick you up this evening and we'll do the town." You didn't cross the perimeter for social calls. The EAM had this disagreeable habit of shooting people in Allied uniform. At night they delighted in lying in ambush beside a road. As you breezed along in your jeep they would pull a rope they had stretched across the pavement and out into the middle of the road would come a land mine. And you'd run over it. So you were wise to stay indoors at the Grande Bretagne of an evening.

However, such was the spirit of *entent cordiale* among the Greek girls that they took it upon themselves to solve this problem. They decided that it would be they who would visit their male friends in the hotel, they would just walk boldly across the perimeter, on the assumption that being in civilian clothes they would not be fired at. This turned out to be a splendid arrangement. After a heavy day of military duties an Allied officer could look forward in the evening to being host in his hotel room to an attractive Greek girl and relax sipping *ouzo* by bootlace-light.

But there was one other slight snag and it was all very ironic. It hinged on the matter of diet. In Italy the troops had been able to augment their drab army food with eggs, chickens, and other produce which they had no hesitation in plundering from the locals, the two-faced, double-dealing wartime Italians for whom they had no respect whatsoever. But in Greece it was different. The Greeks, apart from the EAM baddies, had been on our side right from the outset of the war. There were strict military orders that there would be no plundering, which was something the troops willlingly went along with. This meant, therefore, that our diet was strictly army fare and, as you probably know, it is doctored to hold down the sexual urges of the troops. This gave rise to the terrible situation at the Grande Bretagne Hotel whereby you had men going to the M.O. and saying, "Doc, I don't know what's wrong with me. Last night there was this terrific babe dropped in to see me. It was all set for a memorable evening. But then when we'd got rid of the small talk and it was time to get on with the . . . I dunno, Doc, I'm worried." Somehow or other, however, this bridge was usually crossed. One can do anything, really, if one puts one's mind to it.

These assignations were unusual also when it came to what is normally, "I'll see you home." That was out. The best a fellow could offer was to walk her to the corner of the hotel and say, "Chivalry is not dead, but I will be if I step out into the open there." You felt an awful heel escorting her just the few yards to the sheltered edge of the building and saying your good-nights there, when she then had to set off to the lines of EAM insurgents armed to the teeth and walk past them whistling a happy tune and trusting to luck that none of them would turn nasty.

Is it any wonder, then, that the Greek girls so endeared themselves to those of us fortunate enough to come out alive from the cauldron that was the Greek Civil War?

The American Woman Abroad

The American woman naturally has a chapter to herself (the following one), but here let us deal with this one aspect of her.

Although she is out to please and wants to be liked, the American woman abroad unfortunately is not highly rated.

The Europeans look at her clothes and see that obviously money has been spent there, more than the average local woman has for spending on herself. Everything is immaculately pressed and bandbox fresh. But there is no flair about the way she wears her clothes and—dare one say it?—she looks just a little bit old-fashioned.

In conversation she indulges in what has been called the "rehearsed response." Ask her where she is from and what you are likely to get is: "I was born in Duluth and spent the formative years of my life in California but lately I have been residing on the eastern seaboard." "How do you like London?" "Pending a full appraisal at the conclusion of my sojourn here, I would say that ..." Exaggerated? Only a little. It all pours out like a script.

She seems to the European to lack sensitivity, feeling. It is so hard to get to her, to break through the barrier of conformity to the attitudes of mind and patterns of behavior laid down by her country, to cut through the jargon and get to a real person with her own views and emotions.

This contributes to her not being greatly sought after as a love object, compared say to her French or Danish cousins. "Our relationship has now reached a stage where I feel I should consent to intercourse." That is *not* exaggerated. It is a direct quote garnered when researching young European males with the question "What do you think of American girls?"

In a less-young age group a traumatic experience can befall the well-preserved, well-groomed, well-heeled American woman on her European trip. When the mature (to her way of thinking) American woman is confronted by sex European-style she doesn't quite know what's hit her. She shows a definite inclination to become gaga and schoolgirlish. She is putty in the hands of a Bavarian count or a young sexual athlete of the Sorrento beaches. Not without good reason has she become a stock character of fiction. Sinclair Lewis portrayed her devastatingly in his novel *Dodsworth*, brought brilliantly to life by Ruth Chatterton on the screen. Tennessee Williams depicted her unsparingly in *The Roman Spring of Mrs. Stone*. Movie director David Lean, in *Summertime*, had Katherine Hepburn and Rossano Brazzi epitomizing the matronly American in an embarrassing dither about the suave Continental.

When such as she returns to Milwaukee, or wherever, she is likely to spend long periods looking into space.

Canadian Frigidity or *I Only Have Ice For You*

In Canada, of course, you are getting into the problem of climate. A country which is the wrong way round (it should run north and south instead of east and west), Canada has but a few short months of summer, from June through September. By October there is a sharp nip in the air and from November to the following May you're snowed in. Now it stands to reason that when a woman is encased in about six layers of clothing for that long period she has little opportunity for sexual signaling. What, after all, can be seen of shapely bust, slim waist, or attractively contoured posterior? Also, thus encumbered to keep out the cold, there is a definite shortage of that important ingredient of the male-female association—opportunity. Compare it, say, to the readily-at-hand New Zealand lass in and out of a bikini practically every day.

Allied to this cold climate dampener is the fact that nigh on two thirds of the Canadian population is concentrated in the two provinces of Ontario and Quebec. The latter is one of the great strongholds of Roman Catholicism. Ontario is rabidly Presbyterian. The two are at loggerheads. Ontario's Presbyterians, many of whom travel under the banner of their homegrown United Church, deride the Quebec Catholics with the jibe: "Yours is a very convenient religion. You sin and then just go to confession and everything's all right." To which the Catholics reply: "Perhaps so, but your Presbyterian Conscience doesn't even allow you the fun of sinning."

These divergent religious influences do, however, have one thing in common. They have a similar effect on the behavior and outlook of the Canadian female as a whole. Prudery is a frequently to be encountered characteristic.

England

The English female has long suffered from the fact that there were 2,000,000 more women in the country than men. It was a mathematical certainty that a lot of them were going to wind up on the shelf. It was so sad to see them dancing with each other not only at the local hop but also in more gracious settings.

Her plight was not made any easier by the fact that, not to put too fine a point on it, the Englishman is no great lover. For far too many young Englishmen their idea of a whizbang evening for a girl is to go calling on her with a copy of *Autocar* and read out to her all the exciting details about the new 3.5-litre Jag.

A Frenchman walking with an English friend in a London park was appalled at the sight of all the lovemaking going on, even right there on the grass verges of the footpath as they wended their way through the ornamental gardens. "It's partly a matter of the housing problem," said the Englishman, by way of explanation, "and also, although it's gradually changing, for a long time the average young man here hasn't had his own car." "It is not that," said the Frenchman. "What perplexes me is that always it seems to be the girl who is doing all the work."

The inherent characteristic of the English girl with a man is to feel grateful. Observe the difference between an American couple and an English couple walking along the street. In the States the man takes the woman's arm; in England the woman holds the man's arm. It is a basic difference of attitude toward pride of possession.

During World War II American troops stationed in England didn't quite know what they'd struck. Here were girls so dedicated to pleasing them, so undemanding, so broadminded. "You have an overnight pass? Well, why not sleep in my flat?" And in the morning she would shoot all her week's valued wartime rations of eggs, bacon, and butter seeing to it that he had a sumptuous breakfast. It was in such striking contrast to back home, where it was the man's job to put himself out for the woman.

This warmth toward men which had its roots in the British male shortage has not necessarily persisted to such a degree through to today. In the 1960's the dolly birds, the swinging chicks, came on the scene—"England swings like a pendulum do," as the song had it. Thanks to the mini-skirt, Carnaby Street, and all the other trimmings, the English girl became the trend-setter, the pacemaker, the model to be emulated by Continentals and by Americans. Formerly likable but dowdy, she was now always two inches ahead of everyone else in shortening her skirts, always the first with any new clothes, makeup or hairdo fad.

It was all part of the little revolution whereby England took over from America the pacesetting role in the lighter side of life. The United States had always been the leader in the world of the popular song, stage and movie musicals, youthful fashions in clothes, and other such interests. But while the U.S. turned to getting to the moon and other earnest endeavors, Britain hit the world with the Beatles, the Angry Young Men of the theater, the *Beyond the Fringe* and *That Was The Week That Was* type satire shows. And of course the swinging chicks.

The English girl became bold. She lost her endearing humility.

But having the spotlight turned on you and held there, especially when it is a new experience to you, can have ill effects. As the 1960's gave way to the 1970's, the feeling was growing in Britain that the dollies were getting to be a bit of a pain in the neck. It was going to their heads. They were getting a bit big for their hot pants. More than one young Englishman was getting a bit tired of it. It was as if she was conferring a knighthood on him if she deigned to talk to him.

It became just a little tiresome trying to keep up with this new type of English girl's day-in night-out round of the discotheques, dashing about making sure to be seen where *every-body* is seen, maintaining the with-it image at all times or, like Twiggy, being caught up in the breastless whirl of trendy fashion modeling.

It would not have been so bad if the outward appearance had been matched by an inward change. But it was not long before it became apparent that the wearing of buttock-revealing micro-skirts and crotch-tight hot pants was not necessarily what Desmond Morris terms the use of "sexual signaling devices." Many men frequently were mistaken about this, learning abruptly that the provocative garb did not have an *ipso facto* connection with sex. It was merely an outward expression of the desire to keep in the swing of things, the old feminine compulsion to be up with current fashion. The dollies were not in fact as permissive as the impression they gave. Not on home territory, at any rate.

The fact that a two-week package holiday by the sea in the south of Spain can be cheaper than the equivalent in England (without sun) has meant that the English flock there each summer literally in the millions. And none are quicker to avail themselves of this bargain than the English office girl. And when Miss Steno reaches the sun-drenched beaches of Torremolinos or wherever, an amazing change comes over her. The type of girl who when at home in England is muscle-bound from fighting for her honor suddenly goes crazy. Spanish waiters, auto mechanics, and fishermen who never put to sea can only raise their eyes to the heavens and say, "The English señoritas!" They seem to behave on the basis that it is all right to be wanton if you are not seen to be wanton—*i.e.*, if there is no likelihood of "what the neighbors will think." However, it really does irk young Englishmen in a position to observe what is going on, since it gives them the feeling that they are definitely missing out on something. But the last laugh is often with the Englishmen. A not infrequent outcome of those Mediterranean rave-ups has been that when our girl returns home to life in suburbia with Mum and Dad, one day the front doorbell rings and standing there on the doorstep, with all his possessions in a cardboard suitcase tied with twine, is Pedro. "Well," says he, brightly, "here I am, my English rose."

Which can be terribly embarrassing.

I4   THE GREAT AMERICAN EXPERIMENT

The great American experiment—men putting their women-folk on a pedestal—cannot be said to be an unqualified success. There are many outside observers who feel that it is not even a success.

And it is something to worry about—something that does not augur well for the future—that it is from America, where women have never had it so good compared to other countries, that the main drive for Women's Liberation should come. One would have thought that the experiment of making the woman the family focal point rather than the man (as in the Old World) with its resultant high proportion of discontented women, would have furnished a sufficiently chastening lesson as to what can happen when you start meddling with the natural, age-old *status quo*.

When dealing here with the American woman the net is spread to take in her Canadian neighbor. Canadian women might complain that it is not accurate to do that. I suppose there *is* a difference. American women get to their feet for *The Star-Spangled Banner*; Canadian women stand up for *God Save the Queen*.

Newcomers to America cannot help but be struck by the radically different position of women compared to what they are accustomed to elsewhere. The new arrival at once becomes aware of the indicators. He takes a girl out and when they reach where they're going and he gets out of the car, he is puzzled that she still sits there. Then it dawns on him that she is waiting for him to come around the car, open her door, and assist her out onto the sidewalk. Nowhere else in the English-speaking world, from Inverness, Scotland, to Hobart, Tasmania, is this regarded as an essential requirement. After all, being on the nearside she's closer to their objective and it is logical that she would get out herself, especially since much time and effort is wasted if the locking of the car also has to be gone through. Likewise the matter of a man and a woman together approaching a door. In England if the man gets there first he opens it and if she's first on the scene she opens the door. Which makes sense. But in America the newcomer observes that a woman will stand steadfastly at a door and wait until the man is there to open it for her, no matter how long she may have to wait, while he pays off a taxi or whatever. And again . . . a couple are about to leave a bar, for instance, and instead of both getting from their stools and going over to where their coats are, she doesn't budge until the man has gone and got their coats; then she will consent to getting from her stool for him to assist her into her coat.

In dozens of such ways obeisance is imposed upon the American male, to the extent that an Australian would comment: "Stone the crows, sport, American men are bloody doormats."

To which any given American woman is likely to reply: "We know that the only culture Australia has is agriculture, but there *is* such a thing as chivalry. It is just common courtesy from a man to do such things for a woman."

Granted. But here's the point. The American woman on her pedestal expects more than just common courtesy. Chivalry is not dead. But in this day and age the women of England, say, or Germany have a much more commonsense attitude toward it. They will expect and receive such courtesies as door-opening and so on. But they don't make a production of it. If their man is not conveniently at hand to perform such task they will do it themselves. The American woman, by contrast, will wait and wait to extract from her man the toll of his servility.

When the *Blondie* comic strip was first published in England men were baffled by the fact that Dagwood was always going off to some neighbor's garage to play poker with the boys. To them a garage seemed a very uncomfortable place to try and play poker. But what Englishmen didn't know, since it was alien to their way of life, was that American men have to sneak off furtively to follow such male pursuits—"Al wants me to go over and help him fix his car." An Englishman tells his wife: "I'm playing poker with the boys." And that's that.

On a larger scale and just as incomprehensible to males outside the States is that other offshoot of America's female domination—the goings-on at a convention, known in all other parts of the English-speaking world as a conference. Perhaps it is only right that in its American form it should have a name of its own, for a conference is just what it says, it is not accompanied by the chasing of chambermaids along the corridors of convention hotels, the poking of electric sticks up girls' skirts and other such hijinks. The American male embraces the convention so enthusiastically because it means he can get away from his wife, be free for a while from feminine domination, live it up a little. The hunting trip and the fishing trip afford him similar opportunities. Such excursions into the hinterland by serious hunters and fishermen are one thing, but they would seem to be a minority compared to those using it as an excuse for escape from their wives. The unbiased observer of the American scene notices that invariably in the preparations for such junkets the assembling of the hunting gear or fishing tackle is a lesser consideration in comparison to getting the booze organized. The men of other countries don't need to get involved in such complicated arrangements, since any evening they can just announce to their wives that they are going out to the local pub, *bistro*, *gasthaus*, or *bodega*.

If one would analyze what is regarded by those outside the U.S. as the henpecked situation of the American male, it must be admitted that they have very much brought it upon themselves. It was they who decided to break with the tradition of the man being the focal point and undertake the experiment of having it the other way around. It was they who put woman on a pedestal. It was they who, with the help of the cosmetic and foundationwear industries, have glorified her, only to wind up with a thing of beauty and a jaw forever. For they have found that they have spawned what Philip Wylie called *A Generation of Vipers*. In that book he examined the unhappy results of the American matriarchal society, the ill effects of what he termed Momism. Since then, things have not changed. The ramifications multiply.

When I first went to live in America we had a woman neighbor who had been provided by her husband with what might be regarded as all the good things of life—not only her own car and TV in every room but also every conceivable laborsaving device, rapid-action electric floor polisher, high-speed shirt ironer, all that sort of thing. The result was that she had a great deal of spare time and much of this she devoted to playing golf. She became very good at it. So much that on weekends she used to beat her husband, who had always considered himself no mean golfer. Not that it was any of our business, but my wife felt prompted one day to say to her: "You really shouldn't beat your husband at golf." "Why not?" she asked. "Well," said my wife, "the reason you've become good at golf is because he knocks himself out all week to earn the money to buy all the things that give you the spare time to play. The least you could do on weekends is to let him win." She couldn't see it.

Not so important, I guess. But worse was to come. I was horrified to learn that it was not uncommon for American wives to charge their husbands for sex. This conjured up a frightening picture.

"It will cost you a new stove."

"OK."

"Now, you're not just saying that. You'll let me get one?"

"Yes, yes, a new stove."

"I just can't carry on with this one of ours, we've had it for four years."

"Yes, yes, yes, a new stove. You can get a new stove."

"I've seen the one I want. It's just a matter of you making out the check."

"OK. I'll give you a check. Oh, my God, Beth!"

"Promise now."

"Yes, yes, I promise."

"Cross your heart?"

"I can't stand much more of this, Beth."

"Cross your heart?"

"Yes, yes, yes, I cross my heart."

"All right, lover boy, it's all yours."

Having so much showered upon them by their husbands, gifts placed at the altar of the goddess, it is only natural that the pedestalized American woman should be discontented. The kid who gets everything, presents that are umpteen times better than what others get ("OK, you can have an airplane, but you've got to wait till you're old enough to fly it"), naturally becomes sated, knows nothing of the joy of at last getting something longed for. Likewise with women, as in the Peter Arno cartoon of the woman bedecked in jewels and deep in furs sitting with her husband in their limousine and saying: "You're so nice to me and I'm so bored with it all."

Bent on making his woman happy, the American man sees to it that she gets everything she would wish for personally— clothes in abundance, everything that opens and shuts for her Dream Kitchen, a car of her own, a cottage at lake or sea- shore for summer relaxation, etc. He is also preoccupied with aiming to make it the best of possible worlds for American womankind in general, on the basis that if life is made easier for them—their daily chores simplified and made less irk-some—they will automatically be happier. Unfortunately, however, it doesn't work out that way.

Take, for example, a boon which has turned out be one of the root causes of the discontent of the American female—re-frigeration.

The household refrigerator was invented by an English-man, Jacob Perkins in 1834, and with the American expertise at developing to its full potential something invented else-where (radio, movies, television, and so on), the fridge was brought to its apogée in the United States. Its developers and promoters had the American housewife sold on the idea that a refrigerator was as essential in a household as a stove or a kitchen sink long before women of other countries had been exposed to any great extent to it. So overjoyed were Ameri-can women with what their menfolk had provided for them that they became brainwashed as regards refrigeration. They started and have continued to put into their refrigerators such things as jam (which today is so hopped up on preserva-tives that it couldn't go bad if it tried its darnedest), toma-toes (which need to mature in God's atmosphere), and the remainder of a freshly cooked roast (which shows its disap-proval of the whole matter by drying up its natural juices and converting its fat into frozen lard).

But that, as the saying goes, ain't all. In the *Cosmopolitan* of November, 1970, Selig Neubardt, M.D., told "All You Need to Know About Pregnancy and Abortion" and when discussing the matter of a proper specimen for a pregnancy test pointed out that it should be a concentrated urine sam-pling, *i.e.*, the first passed in the morning, since during the day urine becomes diluted by the intake of liquids. He said that this "before breakfast" specimen "should be collected in a clean container and stored in the refrigerator until delivered to the laboratory."

Ye Gods. It hardly bears thinking about. Husband up early to grab a quick breakfast before dashing off to the office on account of he's got a big day ahead. Goes into the kitchen. "Where's the goddam orange juice?" Oh, no.

From straight refrigeration the next progression was to deep freeze and this further boon which men presented to the American housewife meant that she could cut down her visits to the shops even more—she could buy in even larger quantity and heave everything into her super-fridge and its new offshoot, the freezer.

And has this made her happier? Not a bit of it. By reducing her trips to market, it has done her a very bad turn.

Before refrigeration got the American housewife in its clutches she had to go out each day for provisions and these visits to the stores were good for her. They got her away from herself, out meeting people, instead of sitting at home, enlarging petty worries in her mind, feeling sorry for herself. Her modern freeze-everything refrigerator, in league with her laborsaving devices, has given her even more spare time to be introspective.

It has been interesting to observe the change taking place in English women and their cousins on the Continent as the American Dream Kitchen starts to get a foothold there. Formerly the English housewife had to go out each day to buy small quantities of provisions and although she might have complained to her husband what a chore it was having to do the household shopping, each daily trip was in effect an outing. In the course of her shopping she could meet friends for coffee, or drop into the local pub for a drink if she had a mind to. It is for a good reason that office workers like to slip out for "elevenses"—to refresh themselves mentally in different surroundings among different people. Likewise the housewife got away from the monotony of her all too familiar home. But in England now that the refrigerator has moved out of the luxury into the essential class, as it has been in America for so long, the English housewife is getting far more spare time to feel sorry for herself and is moving toward the discontent of American women.

188 THE INFERIOR SEX

And as if the American male, in his misguided effort to ease the lot of his loved one, hasn't done enough damage to her with refrigeration, he has now inflicted upon her that other monumental non-boon—the supermarket.

America has been having some bad luck with her inventions. Things like the Wright brothers' airplane, Edison's phonograph, and Alexander Graham Bell's telephone have stood the test of time. Not so, however, with other American inventions such as the streetcar, the teen-ager, and the supermarket.

Oddly enough the streetcar was invented by a man named Train. In 1832 G. F. Train invented the first modern tramway system and with electrification in the early part of this century this mode of public transport spread like wildfire throughout the world. Soon there was no city, from up in Helsinki down to Cape Town and all points east and west, that was without its streetcars. But then all of a sudden it was realized that as a method of conveying large numbers of people around a town efficiently it didn't work. It was the great traffic snarler. So the huge transport investment of countries around the world had to be written off and the laborious task started of digging all the lines up out of the streets and scrapping the vehicles. Now the streetcar is to be seen only in odd places here and there. San Francisco has kept some, for sentimental reasons. They have been entirely abandoned in Britain, save for some in service as a tourist attraction in the seaside resort of Blackpool. You can still see them in some backward parts of the Continent. And, oh yes, there are still plenty of streetcars to be seen in Russia. They think they invented them.

But apart from those holdouts, the streetcar has proved to be an invention which, although it seemed to be a great idea at the time, just didn't work.

The same thing is the case with the teen-ager—the American idea that people in their teens should be syphoned into a separate, specific group in society. But we needn't go into detail here in regard to what a disaster that has proved.

Now it is becoming all too apparent that we have goofed with the supermarket. This temple erected by the American male for his goddess appeared at the outset to be a wonderful way of easing her lot in life—a timesaving, convenient, expeditious method of getting her marketing out of the way. But as things have turned out, in trying to make things easier for her, men have in fact done her a great disservice.

It is not so much that her shopping has been depersonalized, although that is bad enough. Instead of the friendly personal contact with her local butcher, baker, or grocer as of old, she has been turned into a wire-basket-pushing robot that flicks provisions from shelf to basket. She has none of the joy of haggling as in the former days of the market square, none of what women like so much—the feeling of achievement at getting a bargain. Granted she gets her bargain from time to time, but it is an "8¢ Off Special" along with all the other housewives, not something she has achieved by personal skill at whittling the price down. A mechanical shopper standing endlessly in line at check-out points . . . have you ever noticed the irked, irritated look on the face of men, who created all this for their womenfolk, when *they* are called upon to get involved in supermarket shopping?

But the ill effects of the supermarket go much deeper than that. Their great evil is that the housewife can now get her traditional role as the family shopper over and done with so quickly, for supermarkets must be the quick way of doing it, otherwise what is their reason for being? Accordingly she is afforded much more spare time. And what does she do with all that spare time?

For the Kate Milletts and Betty Friedans of this world, that's fine. They are given the time to turn their minds to far more worthwhile pursuits than going to stores. But the average woman isn't so well-equipped mentally. Some women try to mop up those floods of spare time by becoming joiners—joining the Literary Circle, the Travel Club, and other Helen Hokinson assemblies. Others take group lessons in Spanish dancing and the "Art of the Castanet" or something equally fatuous. But the bulk of women, let's face it, have merely been presented with time that they do not know how to occupy usefully, so that it becomes time on their hands, time for self-examination and discontent with their lot in life, time to mope, an added incentive to become neurotic.

I feel that the Women's Liberationists would do well not to direct themselves so much toward what they feel are the evils of men in not granting women equal pay and opportunity in industry, commerce, the arts and sciences, and so on, and give attention to the real harm men have done women by such misdirected efforts to make them happier as those outlined above.

15   LOST IN THE FEMINISTS' WORD JUNGLE

Every revolutionary movement must have its literature. In the case of Women's Liberation it includes such books as:

> *The Feminine Mystique*, Betty Friedan (1963)
> *S.C.U.M. Manifesto*, Valerie Solanas (1967)
> *The Sensuous Woman*, "J" (1969)
> *Sexual Politics*, Kate Millett (1970)
> *The Dialectic of Sex*, Shulamith Firestone (1970)
> *The Female Eunuch*, Germaine Greer (1971)

In the main, women in print on the subject of their liberation are very heavy going. One trudges across deserts of turgid wordiness before coming upon an oasis of readability.

A fault common to most of the Women's Lib books is that

their authors have the "Look! I went to college!" approach. In this regard the tome produced by Kate Millett (University of Minnesota and Oxford) is a prime example.

Kate Millett

The thesis *Sexual Politics* has four pages of acknowledgments, thirteen pages of bibliography, and fifteen pages of index. Fair enough. Good documentation. But then we come to the footnotes. In a book of 360 pages of text the footnotes add up to a total of fifty-three pages. Rarely have I ever encountered such a bad case of what someone once called foot-and-note disease. One chapter has no fewer than 235 footnotes. *Ibid* bids fair to be the most used word in the book. At the foot of one page there is a string of eleven *ibids*, followed on the next page by a further ten and eventually there is a total of twenty-four of them in a single four-page section giving credit to Lundberg and Farnham for the stuff she has quoted from their *Modern Woman: The Lost Sex*. Things start to border on the farcical when she gives a footnote credit to Lundberg and Farnham for such things as "emulate the male" and "everything falls into place." Why not just credit the book in the text at the beginning of the section and then even the most stupid readers will know that all the quotes that follow are from that source?

By the time the reader has reached page forty, and the eighty-first footnote, he is saying to himself: "All right, Kate, we've got the message. You went to university. Now get on with the goddam story."

Trying to plow through the reading matter and the 1,078 (by actual count) footnotes of *Sexual Politics* is akin to something like this:

As the dog[1] walked down the street[2] it encountered a cat.[3] The cat decided to "be prepared."[4] It took "evasive action." [5] The ladies[6] who owned the cat called to the man with the dog to put it on a leash. To which the man curtly replied: "Nuts."[7]

[1] Webster's *Dictionary*, p. 96.
[2] *Ibid.*, p. 172.
[3] *Ibid.*, p. 74.
[4] *The Boy Scout Manual*, p. 7.
[5] Montgomery: *A History of Warfare*, p. 36.
[6] *A Guide to the Rest Rooms of New York*, p. 2, *et seq.*
[7] *The Chrysler Book of Spare Parts*.

But, some feminist hastens to interrupt, the book is a best-seller, you can see it right there on the jacket of the later editions: "WORLD BESTSELLER." I am not in the least surprised. In fact I should have been surprised if it had failed to become one. Never has an author culled so many explicit descriptions of sexual gymnastics, normal and abnormal, since the *Japanese Fornicator's Guide of 1827*. It is open to question how many readers have got Kate Millett's message, how many have painstakingly read every word of the book, with their heads bobbing up and down Yo-Yo-like from text to footnotes, rather than just pouncing on what are tradition-ally called "the juicy bits." For those of us trying to get to grips with Millett (I am sure she and the other Women's Lib writers want to be referred to in the good old masculine way, rather than Miss Millett or Mrs. Yoshimura or even Ms. Mil-lett), sincerely trying to get what she was driving at, it has been a hard, even fruitless, task. As a quoter, she is an expert. None better. But as one journeys through her tome one waits and waits for original thought, constructive analysis, reasoned conjecture, and illuminating conclusions drawn by the author herself.

Germaine Greer

Much more direct is Germaine Greer. She has to be. She is an Australian and if she were not direct she would be severely admonished by her compatriots. Australians cannot abide any of their countrymen who don't call a spade a bloody shovel. She has what in its polite form could be called the to-hell-with-you-for-a-start attitude of the typical Aussie, which of course is his way of overcoming his inferiority complex when confronted with the more sophisticated, more worldly ways of the Old World.

It is not without good reason that *The Female Eunuch* shot up to the top of the best seller lists. In its first twenty-nine chapters Greer dealt incisively with the state of women, even if well adrift in many of the conclusions she drew. For example, on page 255: "In erotic writing . . . the great love affairs were those truncated by death . . . the Romantic taste for the moribund heroine is itself a manifestation of sexual disgust and woman-hatred." That really is naive. Before and since *Romeo and Juliet* all writers have known that something dramatic has to happen to their heroine *or* hero if their story is going to capture the reader's (or playgoer's) interest. Who wants to read about a smoothly flowing uneventful love affair?

Elsewhere we go into other such warped contentions by Greer, but here let us deal with her Big Finish, the final chapter headed "Revolution," in which presumably Greer is going to outline how women can rise up against those iniquities visited upon them and by opposing, end them. And what do we find?

This sort of thing:

Most women would find it hard to abandon any interest in clothes and cosmetics, although many women's liberation movements urge them to transcend such servile fripperies. . . . The most expensive preparations in the cosmetic line are in essence no different from the cheapest; no miraculous unguents can actually repair failing tissue. It is well to consider diet and rest for the raw material of beauty, and use cosmetics strictly for fun. The cheapest and some of the best fun are the colours used on the stage in greasepaint. . . . Instead of expensive extracts of coal marketed with French labels, women could make their own perfumes with spirit of camphor, and oil of cloves and frankincense, as well as crumbled lavender, patchouli and attar of roses. Instead of following the yearly changes of hairstyle, women could find the way their hair grows best and keep it that way. . . .

Revolution? This must have got into the book by mistake. Surely it was something Greer wrote for the Beauty Hints column in *Women's Realm.*

Then we get this:

It would be genuine revolution if women would suddenly stop loving the victors of violent encounters. Why do they admire the image of the brutal man?. . . . If women were to withdraw from the spectatorship of wrestling matches, the industry would collapse. . . . We read in men's magazines how the whores of American cities give their favors for free to the boys about to embark for Vietnam; if soldiers were certainly faced with the withdrawal of all female favors, as Lysistrata observed so long ago, there would suddenly be less glamour in fighting. . . .

This sounds more like a revolution. Having put the wrestlers out of business and got the whores organized, we're starting to get someplace.

But wait. What are we onto now?

The chief means of liberating women is replacing of compulsiveness and compulsion by the pleasure principle. Cooking, clothes, beauty and housekeeping are all compulsive activities in which the anxiety quotient has long since replaced the achievement or pleasure quotient. It is possible to use even cooking, clothes, cosmetics and housekeeping for *fun.* . . . It ought to be possible to cook a meal that you want to cook, that everybody wants to eat, and to serve it in any way you please, instead of following a timetable, serving Tuesday's meal or the tastefully varied menu of all new and difficult dishes you have set yourself as a new cross, and if you simply cannot feel any interest in it, not to do it. . . .

Women's Realm has obviously switched her to the Cookery column.

Don't for one moment think that I am purposely picking

out the trivia in the Greer Liberation Manifesto as put forward in her chapter on Revolution. These are the *highlights*.
More of the same:

Women must also reject their role as principal consumers in
the capitalist state. . . . Children do not need expensive toys,
and women could reject the advertising that seek to draw
millions of pounds out of them each Christmas. Some of the
mark-up on soap powders and the like could be avoided by
buying unbranded goods in bulk and resisting the appeal of
packaging. . . .

It really is difficult to take seriously this stuff which is
obviously overspill from the Shoppers' Guide in a women's
magazine.

I don't know about you, but I've had about enough of this
Women's Realm type pap. But let's give Greer a fair chance.
Let's quote from the final paragraph of her book. You know
that final paragraph—that's the one that you really work on,
phrasing it and rephrasing it, determined to get it right, determined that it will be seen to be writing with a capital W. Here
goes:

The surest guide to the correctness of the path that women
take is *joy in the struggle*. Revolution is the festival of the
oppressed. . . . Joy does not mean riotous glee, but it does
mean the purposive employment of energy in a self-chosen
enterprise. . . . To be emancipated from helplessness and need
and walk freely upon the earth that is your birthright. To
refuse hobbles and deformity and take possession of your
body and glory in its power, accepting its laws of loveliness.

Accepting your body's laws of loveliness! What in God's
name does that *mean*?

Let's move on.

Valerie Solanas

Valerie Solanas, author of *S.C.U.M. Manifesto*, is of course a
joy. In print, that is, since her personal behavior is a bit

spectacular for some tastes. Nobody could ever accuse her of
not being incisive, of not presenting constructive suggestions
as to how male domination can be overcome:

If a large majority of women were SCUM [Society for Cutting Up Men], they could acquire complete control of this
country within a few weeks simply by withdrawing from the
labour force, thereby paralyzing the entire nation. Additional
measures, any one of which would be sufficient to completely disrupt the economy and everything else, would be for
women to declare themselves off the money system, stop
buying, just loot and simply refuse to obey all laws they
don't care to obey. . . .

A small handful of SCUM can take over the country within
a year by systematically fucking up the system, selectively
destroying property, and murder. . . .

SCUM will become members of the unwork force, the
fuck-up force; they will get jobs of various kinds and unwork. . . .

SCUM will forcibly relieve bus drivers, cab drivers and subway token sellers of their jobs and run buses and cabs and
dispense free tokens to the public. . . .

SCUM will destroy all useless and harmful objects—cars,
store windows, "Great Art", etc.. . . .

SCUM will couple-bust—barge into mixed (male-female)
couples, wherever they are, and bust them up. . . .

SCUM will kill all men who are not in the Men's Auxiliary
of SCUM. . . .

SCUM will keep on destroying, looting, fucking-up and
killing until the money-work system no longer exists and
automation is completely instituted. . . .

Etc.

Delightful invective, but so impractical as not to be taken
seriously.

Two Little Words—Eight Little Letters

The foregoing prompts me to break off for a moment to
draw attention to a characteristic of the feminists in print—

their peppering of their text with four-letter words, particularly *fuck* and *cunt*. They take full advantage of the fact that these words have, since 1960, become acceptable in print. The year can be pinpointed because, as is not generally known, the *Lady Chatterley's Lover* court case in London in 1960 revolved almost entirely around those two words. Previously in England, and in the rest of the world for that matter, all the other four-letter words had at one time or another found their way into public print, but whenever one or other of these two got onto the printed page the police immediately pounced. Copies were confiscated, publisher and bookseller were haled into court. Penguin Books, prepared to lay out a tidy sum on a test case, decided to go to bat for *fuck* and *cunt*—as to be found in such generous quantities in the pages of the unexpurgated *Lady Chatterley*. As you know, they won the case and the moment the verdict was known at least two London newspapers paraded these formerly offending words. The floodgates were open.

A decade later the feminists decided to embrace them. Among the feminists in print we find: "The implication that there is a statistically perfect fuck . . ." (Kate Millett), ". . . they've seen the whole show—every bit of it—the fucking scene . . ." (Valerie Solanas), ". . . the cunt must come into its own" (Germaine Greer). On one page of Kate Millett's *Sexual Politics* there are fourteen *fucks*, with a couple of *cunts* as makeweight. Clearly this is an attempt to copy men, to show that they are on an equal footing with them. But in this they are misguided, on two counts.

Firstly, why choose one of the less attractive male characteristics as something to ape? If a young man of ambition were trying to emulate a great statesman, say, or writer, or golf pro he would copy the things that made that person great. He most certainly wouldn't copy the fact that he picks his nose. The fact that men throw around words such as *fuck* and *cunt* is not an admirable quality. Would not the feminists be far better employed in trying to emulate the good male qualities?

And secondly, there are many words and phrases which can be designated as essentially male or female. The two under discussion have long been characteristically masculine. They don't sound right coming from women. Which comment would at once prompt the feminists to say, "How prissy! How straitlaced!" But let's put the shoe on the other foot. Supposing a man committed something like this to paper:

Hank Slabbokowsky went up to the coach before the big game and said: "Gee willikins, coach. I've got a frightful tummyache. Daddy says I shouldn't play."

"Heavens to Betsy, Hank. How maddening."

"Not to worry. I'll get in there and do my darnedest."

"Hank, you're sweet. I'm sure you'll play divinely, tummy or no tummy."

Sickening, isn't it? But it is precisely the same thing, in reverse, as women making free with *fuck* and *cunt*. They are two words which have long been alien to the feminine vocabulary—with one exception, which we'll come to in a moment. As regards *cunt*, you may be sure that somewhere in the English-speaking world at any given moment some woman is saying to her husband: "Don't use that word!" And he is doubtless saying: "Well, what do *you* call it?" "Women," she'll say, "don't actually call it anything." This stems from their ignore-it-and-it'll-go-away attitude toward what is the focal point throughout their lives of so much worry and concern for them, from the advent of menstruation through to cystitis, or dread of it. Even when it is quiescent women have disturbing thoughts about it. As Germaine Greer says: "Vaginal secretions are the subject of a vast folklore; the huge advertising campaigns for deodorants and sweeteners of the vulvar area deliberately play upon female misgivings about the acceptability of natural tastes and odours. One vaginal deodorant is even flavoured with peppermint to provide an illusion of freshness and inhumanity. Others are mentholated. The vagina is described as a *problem* preventing some of the niceness of being close." This is a persistent worry which would seem to make women's theme song "Odor, What Can the Matter Be?" and when linked with all the other sources of concern down under, there is every reason why they prefer not to give it a name.

It is not unusual for some women to be well advanced in years before ever even encountering the word *cunt*. With men, however, it is so ingrained into their common usage that you can get the situation whereby a Cockney couple is sitting in front of the fire with their youngster and when the woman starts to feel the effect of the heat her husband turns to her and says: "How many times have I told you not to scratch your cunt in front of the C-H-I-L-D!"

It is not a pretty word. The privately circulated poem attributed to the late A. P. Herbert makes that point:

The portion of a woman that appeals to man's depravity
Is fashioned with considerable care,
And what appears to be a simple little cavity
Is really an elaborate affair.
There's the vulva and vagina
[Etc.]

After listing all the words for it, anatomical and pictur-esque, that are in existence, the poet is left wondering why it is that men choose to use that ungainly word. But an even more famous poet, Shakespeare by name, was not above us-ing it—in his well-known pun in *Hamlet* when he referred to "country matters."

To the male it has long been an extremely useful word, so masculine in its usage that if women, who have always avoided it, try to substitute another word it is as impractical as attempting to find an exact equivalent in English for for-eign words like *décor, simpática* or *hors d'oeuvres*.

The word *fuck* has been in common use by men from away back in medieval times when they adapted it from its original agricultural meaning of "to sow the seed." This, also, they find a very useful word. As an explosive outlet, when

you hit your thumb with a hammer, for example. As an
epithet when giving vent to personal animosity. As a word
which as soon as it is introduced in a joke automatically
makes you laugh and which, if a more polite word is substi-
tuted, at once destroys a punch line. As in the true story of a
college boy playing his first game in big-time football: He
found himself up against a player who was not only one of
the biggest and toughest in football, but was also notorious as
the dirtiest to have taken the field in recent years. No sooner
had the game started than the fearsome one, operating on the
principle that the thing to do is always to establish psychological ascendency, said to the fledgling: "I'm going to grind
your face in the mud." And that was only for starters. He
went on to give further lurid details as to what he was going
to do to him. When the young player was telling his team-
mates about it afterward they asked: "And what did you say
to him?" He replied: "I told him to fuck off. But not very
loud."

But the word has never had similar acceptance with wom-
en. In moments of annoyance they will far more readily blas-
pheme than make use of it. If they pull the cord of the iron
out of its socket and blow the fuses it is far more likely to be
"Christ!" than "Fuck!" There is a subtle difference here. In
her choice of expletive the woman is saying to herself: "Ca-
lamity! How on earth am I going to overcome this situation I
have created?" Whereas the man is merely expressing his annoyance at the waste of time in having to deal with something he can easily cope with. However, although the female
will not bring it readily into use at such times it is embraced
by more than a few women in special circumstances, those
circumstances appropriately enough being associated with
sex. Inwardly, many women are sexually excited by the
word.

Not, of course, from a casual acquaintance, such as a truck
driver who has stopped to ask directions. The setting has to
be just right, the man has to be the Loved One, or candidate
for the role. With the soft lights, mellow drinks, and Sinatra

records getting to him, in mid-embrace on the *chaise longue* he states through clenched teeth in high tension what he would really like to do to her. Immediately into top gear goes her emotion urge and the more he repeats it the more it is music to her ears.

For her part she, too, will readily use the word in an intimate setting, with similar heightening of sexual excitement for the male. As every man knows, "be gentle with me" is all very well, it excites a man because it is flattering to his ego (*he* is the one she has chosen to bring to her life a dramatic change of pace), but it cannot compare as a sex stimulator to a full-throated "Fuck me!" And every woman with a liking for a bed knows that, as with a pilot being talked down, urgently repeated use of the word can talk in a timid lover.

But all that is a private matter. For the feminists to try to bring it into common usage with women, as with men, is to debase it. The woman who calls everybody *darling* takes all the sincerity out of that word. The feminists would do well to leave things just as they are in regard to women's present discriminating and effective use of the word *fuck*.

Shulamith Firestone

Although a founder member of the Women's Liberation movement, Shulamith Firestone cannot be regarded as very important, to it or us. This is brought forcibly home when one tries to read the credo of this Ottawa-born young New Yorker, as detailed in her book *The Dialectic of Sex*. At once one is made fully aware that she is of the "Look! I went to university!" school of writing (in her case Washington University, among other seats of advanced learning). Try this for size:

The assumption that, beneath economics, reality is psychological is often rejected as ahistorical by those who accept a dialectical materialist view of history because it seems to land us back where Marx began: groping through a fog of utopian hypotheses, philosophical systems that might be right, that might be wrong (there is no way to tell), systems that explain concrete historical developments by *a priori* categories of thought; historical materialism, however, attempted to explain "knowing" by "being" and not vice versa.

Sentence after sentence in *The Dialectic of Sex* is a candidate for the "How's That Again?" department of the *New Yorker*:

In the second type of cultural response the contingencies of reality are overcome, not through the creation of an alternative reality, but through the mastery of reality's own workings.

If our direct experience contradicts its interpretation by this ubiquitous cultural network, the experience must be denied.

The coaxing of reality to conform with man's conceptual ideal, through the application of information extrapolated from itself, we shall call the Technicological Mode.

We shall assume this definition of historical materialism, examining the cultural institutions that maintain and reinforce the biological family (especially in its present manifestation, the nuclear family) and its result, the power psychology, an aggressive chauvinism now developed enough to destroy us.

Firestone's *The Dialectic of Sex* epitomizes the type of book of which it has been said: "I couldn't put it down. I was asleep at the time."

The Sensuous "J"

A noticeable feature of the feminists in print is that they are almost entirely humorless. They take themselves *so* seriously, the same earnestness that is to be seen in a female who at last makes it to a seat on the Board. In the dust-jacket puff of her *Sexual Politics* Millett is billed as being a writer "with style

and wit." Style perhaps, but wit—it's a lie. Reading the out-
pourings of the Women's Liberationists one seeks hopefully
for the shaft of wit that would help them to bring home a
point tellingly, but rarely is one rewarded.

A delightful exception to this is *The Sensuous Woman*, the
book in which "J" attempted to liberate women from their
naiveté about sex. Instead of being on the Sex Education
shelves in the bookstores (or under the counter in many),
here is a work which should be displayed prominently in the
Humor section. It is a very funny book. But how much of its
humor is intentional is a moot point, in view of the fact that
it is represented as instructing women how to have "a fulfilling sex life . . . the first *how-to* book for the female who
yearns to be *all* woman."

For example, in her section on what author "J" calls pe-
nis/mouth techniques is "The Whipped Cream Wriggle." She
suggests that freshly whipped cream with a dash of vanilla be
spread on the male member and then licked off, to the great
enjoyment of the partner. She cautions, however, that if you
have a problem with your weight "use one of the many artificial whipped creams now on the market."

If a man had written that, the big laugh in the final sentence would obviously have been a take-off on women's approach to things, but coming from a woman it has the ring of
the sort of thing women say to one another in all seriousness
when the girls are having a hen party over coffee: "I used to
give Gerald the "whipped cream wriggle" regularly but I've
had to give it up since I've gone on the Weight Watchers'
Diet."

For a certainty, however, the author of *The Sensuous
Woman* did not mean to be funny when she penned such
gems as piece of advice No. 3 to women about to attend their
first orgy, "If you're menstruating, stay home."

Funniest, yet without question meant to be taken seriously by the women who eagerly fish the book out from its
hiding place as soon as their husbands go off to work, are
those passages dealing with how to rekindle your husband's
sex interest in you.

Marge, it seems, managed the trick by first having "their conventional bedroom done over in—are you braced for this? —mirrors, smoky mirrors on the walls and ceilings." Then when Ted had a bath when he got home he found attached to a towel an invitation to join Marge in the bedroom. Ted, it appears, was thoroughly intrigued and he went into the mirrored bedroom to "catch sight of Marge stretched out on the fur throw on the bed in a black bikini, her body reflected, reflected, reflected everywhere." Result of this was that "he never left that bedroom for the whole weekend."

Janet's technique was purposely to delay her dressing for a party until the very last minute and then on arrival at their hosts' front door, looking immaculate, she grabbed her husband's arm and gasped, "Oh, Dick, I was in such a hurry, I forgot to put on my panties!" The effect this had on Dick was by all accounts devastating. Do you know that by the time they started for home it had worked him up into such a state about "Janet's tantalizing and secret nakedness that he couldn't wait to make love to her—they stopped off at a motel!"

Sue does it another way. When the children are away on vacation she dresses up in all sorts of costumes to greet her husband when he comes home from work and changes her personality to match her garb. From one night to another it might be "a harem girl . . . Folies Bergère show girl . . . gypsy fortune teller . . . Roman slave girl. . . ."

One shouldn't laugh. The tragic thing is that women actually do such things, to the excruciating embarrassment of their husbands. After all, how would a woman feel if her husband came home one night dressed as Tarzan and on other nights as an Italian gigolo, a ski instructor, an Estonian weight lifter, Bluebeard, an All-American quarterback, and the Sheik of Araby?

Betty Friedan

Since her book *The Feminine Mystique* was first published as

far back as 1963, Betty Friedan may be regarded as the veteran as far as the Women's Liberation propagandists are concerned. So much so that all the TV and public platform.
exposure that publication of her book has brought her has
prompted more than one housewife to say: "Oh my God, if I
have to watch that woman on television again mouthing
those same things over and over again ... !" But I think that
is rather unfair. Like any other pioneer voice in the wilderness, Friedan has had to hammer her message across, even if
that message is more than a little cocked up.

Her grandstand finish in *The Feminine Mystique* was the
chapter headed "A New Life Plan for Women." Sounded
promising, but first one had to wade through a batch of case
histories of suburban housewives who have solved the problem of "the housewife trap" by doing such things as taking
up painting ("I saw an artist painting and it was like a voice I
couldn't control saying 'Do you give lessons?' "), or playing
the violin ("A voice within me said, now is the time, you'll
never get another chance"), or some other kindred activity.

There is certainly no *New* Life Plan about that. Females
trapped in the home have been doing that sort of thing, with
varying degrees of success, since the Brontë sisters started
writing their novels. Before that, actually—away back in the
1790's when Jane Austen was at work on *Pride and Prejudice*
and her other books.

But apparently, according to Friedan, there is something
which prevents the majority of American housewives from
"discovering their own gifts," from writing "poems like Edith
Sitwell ... or finding themselves as Ruth Benedict did in anthropology."

They are not, it seems, getting enough higher education,
which is one of the main planks of the Friedan platform.

"The key to the trap is, of course," says she, "education. ... Among the women I interviewed, education was the
key to the problem that has no name when it was part of the
new life plan, and meant for serious use in society—amateur
or professional. They were able to find such education only
in the regular colleges and universities."

If I may interrupt here I should like to mention that Friedan committed a real blooper when she linked Edith Sitwell with higher education. Edith Sitwell did not go to university. She didn't even go to school, having been "educated privately," *i.e.*, at home. Brother Sacheverell got to school all right, though, and to university. Eton and Balliol College, Oxford. Nothing but the best for *him*. Edith Sitwell would have been much better as an example of discrimination against the girl child and how she triumphed over it. No matter. Let's get back to Friedan's pet theme.

The university is put forward as the answer for women. "What is needed now is a national educational programme, similar to the G.I. bill, for women who seriously want to continue or resume their education." With such measures introduced, then: "Who knows what women can be when they are finally free to become themselves?"

But it is clear that the Friedan cure-all for women, which might well travel under the banner of "We'll get to the top of the tree when we've all got a Ph.D.," does not stand up to logical analysis.

Already in the U.S. for every four men at university there are three women. No one would say that this is an unfair proportion. But on the evidence of achievement it doesn't seem to be doing the women much good. If it were raised to parity, would that mean that immediately, as if by magic, women would start to make a showing comparable to that of men?

Or let's look at it another way. With their more than 3,000,000 students, American women are not only overwhelmingly more university-educated than their sisters overseas; also they are much more happily placed than the *men* in other countries.

Take Britain, for example. Male university attendance there is a measly 150,000. Relating it to population, of every one thousand females in the United States thirty-three are at university, whereas in England of every one thousand males a mere six are university students. But the grossly underprivi-

leged British male manages to muddle through, giving the
world such things as radar, penicillin, the jet engine, television, the hovercraft, and so on, while the American female
has—what *has* she contributed of like importance lately?

Two Kinds of Backlash

There is that quip about the man who said: "I always travel
in Italian ships because they don't believe in any of that
nonsense about women and children first." It has bearing on
the two kinds of backlash that the Women's Liberationists
have brought upon themselves—from men and from women.

A man goes up to a counter in a store and is about to make
his request of the sales clerk when a woman customer brushes
past him, firm in the belief that she is entitled to be served
first. But he turns to her and says politely: "I'm sorry, madam, but I believe in Women's Liberation. You're going to
have to wait." Increasingly this is happening, not only here
but in other parts of the world, not only in stores but in
countless other similar situations. And it is not always politely.

The whole basis of Women's Liberation, as expressed in
Shulamith Firestone's *The Dialectic of Sex*, is: " 'Liberation'
as opposed to 'emancipation' denotes freedom from sexual
classification altogether rather than merely an equalizing of
sex roles." Therefore it is only natural that men should show
a definite inclination to say, "Okay, if you want it that
way . . ."

The perquisites that women have always regarded as their
due by virtue of their sex are manifold. Giving up your seat
for a woman in a bus, for instance. It is no good laughing this
off, no good quoting the story of the young lady standing in
a bus saying to a seated man: "You should give me that
seat."

"I don't see why I should," says he, "I've had a heavy day
at the office and—"

"I'm pregnant."

"Oh, well, that's different." Gets up and gives her the seat. "How long have you been pregnant?"

"Twenty minutes, and am I tired."

The requirement that men should give up their seats to women in public transport, waiting rooms, or wherever is important to the female. It is based on the age-old classification of her as a member of The Weaker Sex. Likewise with the paying of drinks for women and buying them meals—this is away back from the time that man was the sole breadwinner and woman the non-earning homebody. Women are no longer the frail creatures who used to faint at the least provocation and had to be revived with smelling salts, nor are they now all stay-at-homes with no earning capacity. Yet they still enjoy the feminine privileges.

But is Women's Liberation going to change all that?

There is some justification in men saying "You can't have it both ways, you can't remove the differential in jobs, etc., but keep it in your day-to-day life," and speeding up the end of "ladies first" and the feminine freeloading that has been going on for generations.

And there is real worry by the majority of women that the Women's Liberationists, albeit unintentionally, are going to bring about a drastic curtailment of traditional female privileges.

A girl in a crowded restaurant bar sits on a stool given up for her and is into her third installment of the expensive cocktail she chose to have prior to the sumptuous meal that won't cost her a cent. Isn't that immeasurably better than being all alone at home eating a TV dinner? Must I give all this up, she will ask plaintively of anyone who inquires of her what she thinks of Women's Lib.

And it is not just the perhaps logical arrangement whereby the courting male or the husband or any other man who might be expecting favors later should sponsor the food and drink. Any female can get in on the act. The mere fact that she is a female and is *there* when rounds of drinks are being bought means that it is a case of "You mustn't be allowed to pay for anything" from a man who is virtually a stranger to her, with no strings attached.

In this regard women are indeed onto a good thing. Not without reason do so many of them say: "I like it this way. I don't want to be liberated."

This is a recurring theme, one finds, when females are queried about their reaction to Women's Lib.

One is put in mind of militant union leaders who tell their co-workers, "We're going on strike." But often the majority of workers are not in agreement. "We can't hit management for *another* pay raise," they say. "They'll just fold the firm and we'll all be out of work." To which the militants reply "We're going on strike, see, whether you like it or not."

Rarely have militant leaders been so out of tune with those they purport to be fighting for as is the case with the Women's Liberation movement.

Reproduction Ad Absurdum

A striking example of where the Women's Libbers are out of step with the majority of their sex is in their contention that the whole process of reproduction and rearing is degrading to women ("Childbirth is barbaric"—Germaine Greer). The rabid feminist goes on and on about how demeaning it is to look repulsive (*she* feels) during pregnancy and then to be tied—as securely as the tin can to the married couple's going-away car—to the offspring during nursing and rearing. It is terribly unfair, she says, that just because she is a woman she is saddled with this situation, while men get off scot free, to lead full, unhampered lives, enjoy their freedom, further their ambitions.

From this moaning about their lot in life, one would get the impression that women are unique in having this state wished upon them purely and simply because of their sex. But they never stop to think that there are more than a few things that men are doomed to, solely because they are male. While the feminists bleat about the raw deal they get as regards reproduction men could very easily—but don't—complain about how brutally unfair it is that it is they, just because they are males, who are called upon to serve as cannon fodder for their country.

Does the young man just starting up as a lawyer, say, or on the threshold of getting going in business enjoy being drafted? Why, he might argue, should he have his freedom taken away from him, why should he have this interruption in his life forced upon him? More than that, why are he and other males the ones obliged to go into the firing line and be exposed to the possibility of being maimed, disfigured, or killed?

And the interesting thing about these two things which are visited upon women and men solely because of their sex—infant rearing and military service—is that the bulk of women enjoy the former and only a very small minority of men welcome the latter.

Who hasn't time and again been witness to scenes such as the following.

A regular woman customer in the local supermarket remarks to the girl at the check-out counter: "You seem very happy today."

"I won't be working here much longer."

Customer glances down at girl's midriff. "You're not—?"

"Yes. The doctor confirmed it yesterday."

"Oh, I'm so glad for you."

"Thanks. I thought after losing the first one—"

"Oh, you'll be all right this time. Isn't that wonderful!"

You see, it's good news, to be spread around to all and sundry—I'm pregnant! How often over in the men's world does one eavesdrop on something like this: "Gee, Frank, you're on top of the world today. What's it all about?"

"I'll be packing up this job soon."

"You haven't been—?"

"Yes. Drafted. Got my papers in the mail this morning."

"Oh, I'm so happy for you. How does Grace feel about it?"

"She's as thrilled as I am."

One feels that the feminists should stop bucking the tide of general feminine opinion about the offspring bit. One only needs to see how a young woman's eyes light up with pleasure when her marriage moves on to the pregnancy level, how she could bust a bra swelling with pride at any compliment about her kid and what a wonderful job she's doing on it.

It is very difficult to agree with the feminists that that is a degraded woman. This is a weak plank in their platform, the argument that women's role in reproduction is demeaning. But rather than being better occupied in concentration on aspects of liberation about which the majority of their sex agree with them, they persist in trying to find solutions to the "problem" of women having children.

The Test-Tube Baby Situation

To do what they feel is something constructive about combating the "degrading" demands of reproduction and child rearing, the Women's Liberationists naturally embrace the test-tube baby and the day nursery.

If you would read of the very latest developments in the test-tube baby world you can do no better than study the book published just before we were going to press here: *Utopian Motherhood* by Robert T. Francoeur, Associate Professor of Experimental Embryology and Interdisciplinary Studies at Fairleigh Dickinson University. It is hair-raising stuff for the layman, not without its ghoulish aspects.

Apart from going into all the aspects of what may be regarded as the conventional test-tube baby (*i.e.*, one which comes into existence by means of AID, artificial insemination by a donor), Dr. Francoeur goes into the more frightening territory of the EMO, the extra-corporeal membrane oxygenator, "the contraption about the size and shape of a quart juice can" with which a foetus can survive outside the body. We learn from Dr. Francoeur that "the EMO artificial womb has supported life in three dozen lambs for up to two and a

half days, the world record as of spring 1969." But you may
be sure that now we are in the 1970's that is a world record
that the embryoscientists have long since bettered. However,
there is the third category which Dr. Francoeur deals with
and which is the ultimate in the test-tube baby—what is
called *in vitro* (literally "in glass") fertilization. That is to
say, entirely outside the body an ovum is fertilized by sperm,
in a glass artificial womb. Now, as the Women's Liberationists
would say, you're talking! Isn't this the answer? Here is the
elimination of the "demeaning sight" of a woman walking
about heavy with child.

"Dr. John Rock, author of *The Time Has Come*, pio-
neered further work with human eggs in the 1940's," writes
Dr. Francoeur. "Working at the Boston Hospital for Women
with Miriam Mentkin, John Rock cultured human ovarian
eggs *in vitro* for twenty-four hours to induce them to mature. . . . The mature eggs were then cultured for another
forty-five hours in the presence of sperm. Altogether four of
the 138 eggs cleaved into two and then three cells. Whether
these eggs were actually fertilized is still open to question
today . . ."

Time passes. . . . "By 1968 when complications with the
egg had been mainly resolved," Dr. Francoeur continues,
"scientists turned their attention to the sperm. What is the
trigger, the key that capacitates a human sperm so that it can
fertilize an egg? Edwards [Dr. R. G. Edwards of Cambridge
University] and his co-workers tried a number of approaches.
They washed human sperm, aged them with uterine tissues
and bits of fallopian tubes, and then tried to fertilize some
eggs. Of the ninety eggs they used at this time only seven
showed any sign of being fertilized."

So it would seem obvious that it is going to be some time
yet before they've got the bugs out of *in vitro* fertilization. In
the meantime there is tried and true AID, which Dr. Francoeur says most Americans do not realize is "the rather common practice of artificial insemination." He says that many

Americans today react with the same smiling benign incredulity as did Frenchmen more than a hundred years ago when Diderot recorded in *The Dream of d'Alembert*: "A warm room with the floor covered with little pots, and on each of these pots a label: soldiers, magistrates, philosophers, poets, potted kings. . . ." With the benefits of modern science at our disposal we are in fact taking this right out of the dream class. We are moving toward the reality of a woman being able to go to the "Baby Bar" in her local supermarket, and there could be seen all the test tubes lined up on the shelves. There would be a wide choice, as she could see from consulting the labels:

NORDIC TYPE: magnificent physique, Mr. Universe runner-up
WELL-KNOWN MOVIE STAR: specializes in great-lover roles (only one to a customer)
INTELLECTUAL: Professor of English, tweedy pipe-smoker, fond of long walks and listening to symphony records
ROCK SINGER: former lead guitarist of the Pot Hunters and other groups
YOUNG POLITICIAN: voted in college as Man Most Likely to Become President
This Week's Special: TRIPLETS for the price of TWINS

If you think that is outlandish you are obviously not in touch with what is happening in the embryoscientific world. Dr. Francoeur discloses that already rates have been set for donors at "ten to twenty-five dollars for each semen sample." And regulations have been laid down as to "a policy of donor anonymity, to eliminate the risk of the wife transferring her affections to the donor, and the desire to protect the donor's reputation (think of the repercussions for his family if his adventures in paternity became common gossip!)."

One could well imagine the sort of repercussions that would be likely if a donor did not keep his activities strictly to himself. For example, a scene in the home of "HAPPILY MARRIED MAN, fond of children, dog lover, keen gardener":

"You're going to have to give up your sparetime job, Irving. You're so tired. The very life seems drained out of you."

"Wouldn't you be tired? Big Circle Stores have me on special-offer next month and they want to really stock up."

"All right, dear. Turn the light out and we'll get to sleep. We'll try again tomorrow."

Supermarket purchases from the "Baby Bar" would take all the hit-or-miss aspect out of pregnancy. It would not be necessary to use your test tube at once. Women's Liberationists could keep them in the freezer, to be brought out when it was felt that a pregnancy could be fitted into the many other calls on their time. Dr. Francoeur tells us that "at the University of Michigan, Dr. S. J. Behrman and associates reported twenty-nine successful pregnancies with sperm frozen for over two-and-a-half years."

And—something which could not help but appeal to the adherents of Women's Lib—it could be used in conjunction with the latest techniques which would make it an odds-on bet that the new offspring would be a girl. Dr. Francoeur writes: "In the spring of 1970 Dr. Landrum B. Shettles drafted a simple, safe, inexpensive, do-it-at-home technique which, on the basis of his own clinical experiences, should produce an offspring of the desired sex eight or nine times out of ten." Apparently it is all based on the different behavior of gynogenic (female producing) and androgenic (male producing) sperm. The gynogenic sperm are "the fast swimmers, more favored by an absence of orgasm," which makes them ideal for test-tube use. If a girl is required, "Shettles' procedure calls for a minimum of equipment: a seven-dollar glucose fertility test-tape kit, a douche kit, and either a bottle of *white* vinegar or a box of baking soda." Increasing the odds for a girl calls first for "an acidic douche of two tablespoons of *white* vinegar in a quart of water . . ."

It is not long before Dr. Francoeur interrupts himself to say, "Since this is beginning to sound like science fiction. . . ." Science fiction? It sounds more like "How To Get Rid of Those Dried-in Stains." But if you feel you have a pressing need to learn all the details, before we go on to day nurseries we can pop out and get Francoeur (published by Doubleday & Company, Inc., $6.95). And don't forget the vinegar. *White* vinegar.

Day Nurseries

One of my favorite moments while researching this book came when I telephoned one of the most militant of the feminists to ask for an interview. A man whom I assumed to be her husband answered and said: "I'm afraid I'll have to get her to call you back. She's putting the baby to bed."

I felt that this put the whole thing in a nutshell.

Here was a young woman whom I had heard expounding Women's Lib at a party—you know the type, who buttonhole you in a corner and shower you with feminist propaganda and canapé fragments. I realized that it must be infuriating for such as she that the full flood of her militancy must be checked while she attends to conventional female responsibilities. Everything stops for "Coochie, coochie, coo!"

They are the ones who are so vociferous about day nurseries, how they must be set up on a grand scale so that married women can dump their kids and lead the unfettered life of men.

This, to me, is perhaps the most cockeyed attitude for the feminists to adopt. On the one hand they say that the whole process of reproduction and rearing is degrading to women. But with this day nursery solution to what they say is a feminine problem they advocate something even worse. They would turn women into nothing more nor less than, to put it bluntly, fucking machines. A woman would be something into which a penis is inserted; in due course a baby is produced; it is at once whisked away and put into a rearing factory and then, when old enough not to be an hour-to-hour encumbrance to its mother, it would be allowed to join the family circle. If the normal having and rearing children is degrading, how much more so this plan to turn women into baby-producing animals.

And it isn't as if day nurseries on a highly organized basis have proved themselves. The experience in Russia and Israel, for example, shows shortcomings such as these:

●Jealousy of mother toward a person in a day nursery to whom a child may build up an attachment.

●Products of day nurseries are seen to be much better adjusted than other children *in a crowd, i.e.*, more socialized, but they tend to identify collectively and are less well-adjusted as individuals.

●When the day nursery child is in trouble, to whom does he or she turn? They are bewildered by persons with shoulders to cry on coming at them in shifts, whoever happens to be on duty at the time. No *one* person to focus their worries upon like the traditional mother.

●The difference between day nursery and mother care is the difference between the supermarket and the local store—impersonal, not individual attention.

But who, you might well say, am I to stand in judgment on the system? So let us hear from an expert. A news item of September 12, 1971 from Israel:

For three generations, women in the Israeli kibbutzim have enjoyed most of the advantages which the women's liberation movement is striving for. But Dr. Menachem Gerson, head of Research on Kibbutz Education at Oranim, Israel, reports that many of the women are dissatisfied and deeply disillusioned.

Since every woman has a job, there is full economic equality. The kibbutz system enables a woman to do justice to both her job and her family tasks without fear of losing her employment during pregnancy or of her children being neglected while she works outside the home.

Household tasks have been reduced to a minimum: cooking, laundry and mending are provided for by the kibbutz. The remaining domestic jobs are generally shared by husbands.

But many of the older kibbutz women complain that their jobs are too strenuous or too boring. Despite their freedom of opportunity, kibbutz women are less active than men in fulfilling influential tasks and are less vocal than men at decision-making meetings.

More puzzling, perhaps, are the attitudes adopted by the younger women. They are inclined to marry earlier (the average is twenty years of age) than the last generation. They place more emphasis on the wedding ceremony and they have more children (average of three, compared with 1.5 in the founder generation). And they are less willing to delay starting a family before completing their vocational training.

Among the younger women, involvement in their jobs seems to be weaker than are family considerations. Where job and family interests conflict, preference is given to the family.

There is deep dissatisfaction, Dr. Gerson says, among kibbutz women who discarded their traditional role only to find that the fulfilment they expected did not materialize.

But perhaps America's Women's Liberationists feel they can do better than the Israelis. Perhaps their attitude is that Israelis are good enough at six-day wars but when it comes to children and how to get them organized it is the expertise of the good old U.S.A. which will show the world how it can be done.

I wish I had their faith.

16 THE MYTH OF EQUALITY

Of all living creatures the human female is the only one which wishes to change her relationship with the opposite sex.

A doe, a deer, a female deer, as Julie Andrews sang it, has never shown any inclination to swap places with the stag. She is quite content to nibble grass with the girls, look after her young, and strike attractive poses for the tourists in the national parks. Why go around trying to prove your manhood, bashing your antlers together like footballers in the line?

The seal is quite satisfied to bask in the sun and teach its young to swim. Who wants to try to be beachmaster, with all that fighting and getting covered with scars?

But the feminists of the human animal say that it is not right just to be subordinate like that. Males and females are equal, they say.

Try to tell that to a cow. If you did, the sort of answer you would get would be: "Equality of the sexes? Pshaw! Just look at Randy Ralph over there. Strutting about with his nostrils flaring. Rampant at the drop of a hint. After every cow in sight. And look at me. I can't even raise a trot in case I trip over this undercarriage of mine. But that's all right. I'm quite satisfied to just sit here chewing cud from one milking time to the next."

The point is that along with all the other females of the animal kingdom, cows are quite content with their lot in life. Who ever heard of a neurotic cow?

This of course will bring an outburst from any feminist

within hearing. "How dare you compare women with cows!" But it is the most appropriate comparison one could make. Among all living creatures it is cows and women who share a unique characteristic. They are both clearly mammiferous at all times.

"At all times" is the operative phrase. The females of countless species are noticeably mammiferous when with young but for everyday life their *mammae* are so retractable as to be hardly distinguishable from those of the male members of their species. This is borne out by the fact that even the experts at the zoo are constantly flummoxed as to the sex of numerous types of animals and we can even be hoodwinked by domestic pets.

But with women and cows (which have been conditioned that way) their perpetually full-breasted state leaves no question as to their sex.

There, however, the similarity ends since all cows are satisfied with being secondary to the male, as is the case with all other female members of the animal kingdom. They have never given any evidence of having militants among them. Dame Nature in her infinite wisdom *did* create two species which are exceptions. Witness the queen bee, and the anopheles mosquito (of which the female is the exclusive carrier of malaria). Nature brought into being just two animal species in which the female dominates—one for good and the other for evil—and then let it go at that.

Cutting right across what is the generally accepted male-female relationship among living creatures, the feminists wish to alter the balance. In their behalf it might be argued that they are merely trying to put to rights what they feel is men taking advantage of women, becoming too dominant. In the complex society Man has created—as against the simple, straightforward life of, say, the lioness and her lion—the feminists feel that a wide range of opportunities have been built up for the male to discriminate against and exploit his opposite number. They regard themselves as not getting a fair crack at them, as hard done by.

But let us examine two of the basic female desires for equality—equal opportunity and equal pay.

Equal Opportunity—By Legislation?

An interesting thing about the feminists' fight for the right of women to work at men's jobs is that it is the nice clean jobs that they are always after. Women must be allowed to qualify as lawyers, architects, etc. One never hears of them demanding the full privilege of being allowed to work beside street cleaners, sewermen, and plumbers, for instance. There is a great shortage of plumbers. Have you tried to get hold of one recently? Here is a field where women could really move in and dominate. But I have never heard of a woman fighting for her right to work, with equal pay, beside a man clearing a clogged drain.

They do in Russia? Care to go and live in Russia?

We shall accept the fact that women's fight for equality of opportunity does not apply to the unsavory jobs, which *have* to be done and which men are willing to undertake. But in the less messy job world and among what are regarded as rewarding and even exciting occupations, equality of opportunity is just not practical. Take just three spheres as examples—law, music, and air travel.

In law—one eminent judge: "The public still appears shy of entrusting its fate to a woman." British legal writer Fenton Bresler: "Women are charming, adorable, intelligent—but on the whole don't have the masculine kind of intelligence that is required at the Bar. 'My Lord, what I really feel in this case is . . .' I once heard a young girl barrister say. But the judge stopped her. 'Miss ———,' he said. 'Perhaps it is just as well that I don't tell you what *my* feelings are!' She should have known better. She should have known that no barrister expresses in court his own feelings or his own opinions. They are irrelevant. His duty is to present the facts." A law society publication: "It is alleged that there is a disinclination to take women in case they leave at a later date for domestic reasons.

Competition is fierce. Why should a young man whose life-work will be in law be refused in preference to a pretty young girl who, after a few years, will most probably get married and give up practice?"

In music—that great conductor and wit Sir Thomas Beecham once said: "If you put a woman in an orchestra and she is unattractive, the men don't want to play beside her. If she is beautiful, they can't." In symphony orchestras they seldom get beyond the harp, the plucking of which is the intricate, finicky sort of work at which women are traditionally adept, like knitting. When it comes to a good blow in the woodwinds or a hearty bash among the tympani, they haven't got it. Even the really hard labor of pounding away at a lengthy work for the piano is a bit demanding of them. And at the piano they don't look right. A young woman concert pianist put it to me this way: "When a man walks on to the platform in his tails he's got it made. He looks great in that gear and he knows it. The flicking of the tails up behind him as he seats himself on the stool, shooting his cuffs, all the trimmings laid on. But us women in our dresses. You're half way through the Emperor Concerto and a shoulder strap slips. Do you fish your hand in and hoist it up or just let it hang there uncomfortably? Either way it's on your mind and you're not concentrating properly."

Women pilots—the fact that the big airlines do not employ them does not stem from a basic anti-feminine attitude such as in the Stock Exchange and other strongholds of the "man's world." Women have long since proved themselves capable of handling all types of aircraft with efficiency, good judgment and courage, from the days of Amelia Earhart and Amy Johnson, ferry pilots during World War II, and so on. The big airlines would be only too willing to put them in the pilot's seat and some of the smaller airlines do in fact employ them in that capacity.

But there are two main reasons why the major international airlines just can't take them on.

The first is that old feminine bugbear menstruation. With a

couple of hundred passengers on board you couldn't very well have a woman pilot announcing: "Sorry about this wobbly course I'm flying. It's these damned cramps. They'll pass in a minute or two. I hope." As a safety precaution the women pilots would have to be grounded during their periods of inefficiency and this would complicate things for those in charge of the scheduling of flights. It is not an insurmountable problem, since in other spheres it has been possible to work out arrangements to cope with the disruptive influence of menstruation. But the other reason for not having women pilots is far more important.

The captain of a big international airliner is far more than just the fellow in charge of the flying of the plane. On foreign soil he has to be a diplomat. Complications have arisen during the plane's stop at, say, an airport in the Middle East. He has to be able to handle with authority the discussions with the local authorities. In the Arab countries women are treated as Nothings. A woman pilot, despite her impressive World-Wide Airlines uniform, would remain in the eyes of the locals merely a woman, and therefore demanding of no respect whatsoever, a person of no authority. In numerous other parts of the world women pilots would come up against this same type of disrespect. The international airlines could not entrust their aircraft to pilots who on the ground would be kicked around in that way.

One cannot help but feel sorry for women in this regard. The flying of aircraft is one field in which they have proved themselves capable of holding their own with men. Pan Am, say, or BOAC couldn't do anything but agree that any qualified woman, provided she hasn't got the Curse, can handle an airliner as well as a man. But then, to the frustration of females, this extraneous consideration stops us, this matter of how certain other countries regard women. And what can a woman yearning to be at the controls of a jumbo jet do about it? Absolutely nothing.

Which brings us to a basic flaw in the approach of Women's Lib—the view that by getting legislation passed and regulations changed whereby barriers against women are lifted the female millennium will be achieved. This falls down for two reasons.

In the first place you have that perfect example of women pilots, where no amount of legislation giving women full opportunity is going to change things, because of extraneous circumstances on which no influence can be brought to bear.

And second, the point which I brought out earlier. Why all this concentration on opening up spheres for them when in fields which have always been open to them they have achieved either very little or nothing? Poetry, painting, philosophy, invention, songwriting—we have gone into detail about these and the other opportunities of which women have not availed themselves. It is not to their discredit that they have not done anything where they have had every chance to do something. Women don't *have* to be inventors if they have no inclination in that direction. What I maintain is that the Women's Liberation movement is adrift in thinking that if barriers are removed there will be a fundamental change in women and all of a sudden they will take unto themselves the same sort of drive that has got men where they are.

Equal Pay for Women (With Time Off to be Feminine)

Nobody is going to question for one moment that a woman working beside a man, on piecework or rate-for-the-job employment, doing precisely what he is doing, should get equal pay.

But the broad matter of equal pay is not as simple as that. If women are to get "equal pay for equal work" it would in many cases be grossly unfair to men, because so often "equal work" doesn't mean what it says. It does not take into account "unpaid overtime," the hours in which a vast amount of office work is done. It is imposed by employers and accepted by employees that a great deal of work will be done beyond the stipulated 9:30 to 5:30, or whatever it may be.

Male staff do not shy at this because they know that if they did, then those willing to stay on would be regarded by the bosses in a much better light when it came to promotions. This applies also to work taken home, which represents a huge amount of unpaid work done by business employees. Women on the staff, however, can with impunity opt out of working late at the office and taking work home. They can say: "So sorry, I have a husband and two youngsters I have to see to . . . I have to dash to get to the shops before they close . . . and at home I have to prepare their meal and look after them in the evening." So, under "equal pay" terms a woman would accept her $X a week for a strictly adhered to eight hours a day and the men would be getting the same $X for working eight hours plus the hours of unpaid overtime.

If equal pay were universal, male office workers could rightly complain that women had privileges they could not demand for themselves.

This imbalance already exists. Many executives have to contend with the problem created by a mistakenly benign boss giving subordinates equal pay and the male ones being discontented about going home laden with work while the female ones stop at knocking-off time and trip off empty-handed.

And the worst aspect of this is that often as not the feminine employee has not the justification that she has husband and children to think about. Single, she "just doesn't see why" she should take work home, which places the executive in a tricky situation. He cannot force her to, since doing unpaid overtime is not a right which employers can demand but merely a convention. Men do it through desire for advancement and fear of being passed over or losing their jobs if they don't. The average single girl in an office is not similarly motivated. She can adopt the what-the-hell attitude of "I'm going to be leaving to get married soon anyway" and there is no real control one can exercise over an employee in that frame of mind.

There is a basic reason why women must accept the fact that equal pay for equal work cannot have universal application. Whether one enters business, industry, or a service (transport, say) there is a high proportion of jobs which require some sort of training, which means that the employer is not getting full value for money during that period and can even invest a considerable sum in preparing the new employee for full work (business courses, trade schools, etc.). Although there are of course "drop outs" among men, it can normally be assumed that the employer will eventually get the benefit of the time and money invested in the grooming of a male member of the staff. But a female on the staff can, and so often does, announce all of a sudden that she is going to get married or have a baby and pack up. The lower rate of pay she receives is merely the compensation she is paying the employer for the privilege of leaving him in the lurch.

Women's Magazines

It is farcical for women to talk about equality, to plead to be regarded on an equal footing with men, when month after month they stress how different they are through the women's magazines. In their millions they buy them, whether it be *Good Housekeeping*, etc., in America, *Woman's Own*, etc., in Britain, *Elle*, etc., in France, *Brigette*, etc., in Germany, and proclaim in effect: "I am not a thinking person. I am a woman, preoccupied with fashion, beauty, recipes, diapers, knitting, 'Pregnancy Discomforts' and 'Breast Soreness.' "

While women allow themselves to be engulfed in this tidal wave of femininity that rolls from the printing presses, men have more important things to do and to think about. They feel no need endlessly to read about themselves being men— "Your Morning Shave Can Be FUN" ... "Have You Tried the New I-Don't-Know-I've-Got-It-On Jockstrap?" ... This Month's Health Article: "The Disappearing Erection."

There *are* magazines devoted to men's hobbies—motoring,

sports, looking at photographs of nude women. But while one can rattle off the names of women's magazines *ad nauseam*, one is hard put to it to think of a single magazine which is the male equivalent of the women's periodicals. In various countries it has been tried and died of disinterest. The point is that men just don't want to know. For them, being a man is not a career in itself. They have to buy clothes, have haircuts, shave, be fatherly to their children, fix things up in the home and so on. But all those things are secondary to their work, to getting on with what they feel is their true function in life. But for the bulk of women—clothes, cookery, make-up, diapers, concern about feminine ailments, and so forth constitute a way of life in itself. And the women's magazines are there in profusion to give them guidance.

There is no harm whatsoever in women immersing themselves in feminalia. But they cannot have it both ways. They cannot constantly bring renewed interest to the repetitious twaddle purveyed by the women's magazines and then say: "We must be given equality with you men."

If "repetitious twaddle" should raise the hackles of any feminine reader of this, I should mention that I say it not merely from a cursory glance at some women's magazines in a dentist's waiting room.

In my nonage I worked for some years in that field, having been hired by an Editorial Director on the basis that "these goddam women are driving me crazy and it'll be your job to tell them to for Christ's sake stop flapping, the mag will get to press okay." As I say, it was some years ago, but still indelibly imprinted on my mind. Not only my function of virtually patroling the corridors saying "Now now, girls, take it easy, we'll get the magazine to bed all right." But also typical employees such as the Beauty Editor, who had long been in the business but was still convinced that type was made of rubber. Ask her to delete six inches of over-matter from a story and she would cut four inches and say: "That'll be okay, you'll find. Just get the printers to squeeze it up." And the delightful young ninny who, when asked to lift some recipes to plug up a last minute hole in an issue, brought chaos to kitchens across the nation because, as she explained: "I didn't want us to be accused of plagiarism, so I changed the quantities."

Time goes by and now, after my erstwhile close association with them, I take a look at the women's magazines of today for the purposes of this book. And I find that it is the same old stuff . . . except for an attempt to break away, spearheaded by *Cosmopolitan*.

What happened was this. As the 1960's were coming to an end, it looked as though old-fashioned *Cosmopolitan* was doing the same thing. Falling circulation, dwindling ad revenue, the sad familiar story that had seen the demise earlier of such magazines as *Collier's* and the *Saturday Evening Post*. However, to administer the kiss of life to *Cosmopolitan*, in was brought as new editor Helen Gurley Brown. It was certain that the publication would be changed. She had written a book called *Sex and the Single Girl*. Wow!

Indeed there were changes. Up went the eyebrows. Phone calls. "Madge! Have you seen what's happened to *Cosmo*!" It became known variously as "the Women's Lib mag," "the new permissive type of woman's magazine." The operative word was "outspoken."

And, by jove, it was outspoken. It called them *breasts*, none of your euphemisms like bust, bosom, or chest. There were articles on *orgasm*. *Masturbation* got its mention. *Clitoris* peeked up from its pages.

But on close study some interesting points emerged about the revamped *Cosmopolitan*.

There had not been the radical change of deciding to regard its readers as thinking people, worthy of something more profound than the usual women's fare. Perhaps its publishers were wise in this. *McCall's* and *Ladies' Home Journal* had some years previously made the experiment of competing with the general magazines for the memoirs of political leaders and such like. It had not been a success.

What *was* different in the new *Cosmopolitan* was that they

came out into the open about the feminine preoccupations—
the irrevocable step ("Can a Girl Still Be a Virgin in the
1970's?"), pregnancy, abortion, female sexuality ("Normal
Girls Reveal Their True Responses During Lovemaking"),
how to get a man ("What To Do When He Won't Marry
You"), how to keep your man, unwed mothers (which they
didn't title "Carry Me Back to Old Virginity") and menopause (which might have been but wasn't headed "A Change
Is As Good As a Rest").

Two things were clear about what had been done by *Cosmopolitan*, and other women's magazines which had followed
their lead (*Nova* in Britain had more than a few provincial
housewives feeling sick at the stomach at some of the gory
feminine details they went into).

First, they had stuck to the time-honored formula of wom-
en reading about themselves and had merely treated it per-
missively.

And second, it was only an iceberg operation. At the tip
was this material that had never been handled that way previously in women's mags, but the remainder, the big proportion of the iceberg, was the same old cosy stuff that grandma
had been reading in the *Delineator*.

You know the sort of thing:

Sophisticated, worldly Helen Gurley Brown writing in her
    editor's-chair column about going off to see her "mama in
    Osage, Arkansas" (why are female journalists forever writ-
    ing about going home to see Mom?) . . . and how *Cosmo*
    now has an emblem to vie with Esky of *Esquire* and Mr.
    Eustace of the *New Yorker*—yep, it's Lovey, *Cosmo*'s cat.
Beauty Secrets by Fifty-three of the Nicest Witches (Barbra
    Streisand: "I'm oily when I wake up, so first I wash my
    face . . .")
Anatomy of a Migraine
How To Do a (Professional) Paint Job—The Economical Way
    to Razzle-Dazzle Up a Room
The Care and Handling of Cleaning Women

A Day with Elizabeth Arden
(To keep advertisers of beauty products happy, which women's magazines have to do with frequent puffs, out is trotted that old one about sending a drab member of the staff to spend a day at a beauty salon and see the startling results at the end of it ... all about having an egg mask put on ... "How many eggs must the beautiful hens lay per week for the beautiful customers of Elizabeth Arden?" ... "The pedicure lady appeared with a footbath full of warm water and I decided not to tell her that the mere thought of anyone touching my toes, any attempt to pedicure my tootsies, sends me into gales of giggles" ...)
So Nice Around the House—A Wardrobe of At-home Clothes Suited to Your Very Special Life Style

In the course of my research into the so-called New Wave in the world of women's magazines certain young ladies I discussed it with said that I was being unfair, that I had chosen copies of *Cosmopolitan* that were not representative. I pointed out that I had picked the very latest issues, so that by the time this book came out it could at least be said that it was up-to-the-minute at time of writing. They rushed off and duly returned with back numbers which they opened in front of me and said: "What do you think of that!" I then realized that *Cosmo* was starting to run out of things to be permissive about. That is the drawback when you go in for that sort of thing. Anyone who has ever made a blue movie knows that hanging over one is the hampering thought that it has all been done before.

Not the least interesting aspect of what I suppose one could call the "*Cosmo* Experiment" was that the advertisers did not seem to have got the message. Although on its permissive pages the Editorial Department were going it hammer and tongs, the advertisements showed no similar inclination to hit the pregnancy-abortion-masturbation trail. The ads seemed quite divorced, in another world, from what was happening alongside them. On one page screamed the headline:

"ORGASM! What It Is and What It Isn't!" And on the opposite page you were likely to find: "PYREX means you'll never taste yesterday's tuna casserole with today's cherry cobbler."

Seemingly oblivious to what was going on around them, the advertisers were still churning out their age-old full-color mouth-watering food pix, the misty pastel-shaded bath fragrance ads, shampoo and makeup plugs, bras and girdles, boosting your bust, slimming the other parts . . . nothing appeared to have changed, save for more and better adman's jargon, such as a new lipstick being "hyper-allergenic, unscented and dermatologist recommended."

Hidden away in one corner I did find an advertisement for the unhappily named douche, Wild Cherry, which "is not a strong astringent medical-smelling douche . . . nor is it a joke, intended to make you give out with nervous giggles . . . it provides the new sexual freedom." Which I guess can be regarded as an advertiser's nod toward today's Permissive Society.

But the only example I could find of the big advertisers in the women's magazines getting really permissive lay in the fact that now the makers of sanitary napkins have seen fit to display the packages with lid off, so that you can actually see the contents! *That* is a definite breakthrough.

Women's Magazine Fiction

With liberation are we to take it that women would be freed from the acres and acres of mindless feminine fiction which they lap up month after month and with which even *Cosmopolitan* has not been able to make a clean break?

In the course of being fiction editor of a women's magazine I was to learn that there were only nine basic plots, which were used over and over again in various disguises. Knowing this helped me greatly in whipping through the piles of manuscripts I took home in the evening and on weekends.

The standard story is some twenty pages of typescript and I could scan the first page or so ("Oh, yes, good old plot No. 7"), turn to page sixteen, where the writer always comes to the high point, then look at the ending, and in that way get a good idea of whether or not the author had brought sufficient freshness in her treatment of the faithful old plot for the story to be bought.

Three of these stock women's magazine fiction plots which I remember are:

1. *Fabulous Holiday.* This is the one about the girl on vacation at a really sumptuous resort hotel. She meets and falls in love with Dream Boy and her days in the sun with this rich young man are ecstasy. Then on the last day she has to make her confession to him. She is not the daughter of a well-to-do family that he thought she was. She is merely a humble office secretary who saved up all her money (a Hershey bar for lunch each day and that same mended and remended slip for a year) so that she could have this fling. She is not One of His Sort and must now come down to earth again. "Don't worry that lovable little head of yours, Judy," says Dream Boy. "I'm only a lowly paid bank clerk. I, too, saved up all my money for a fling here at the Hotel Splendide . . ."

2. *Reunited.* This is the one about the separated couple whose son, of which our heroine has custody, goes off to a boys' camp or some such place and has a terrible accident. Rushed to the local hospital, he is there hanging to life by a thread. Mother has hastened there, of course, and shortly there arrives the estranged husband. Their shared vigil is rewarded by the doctor's "Your boy is going to be all right." Our heroine's hand meets hubby's on the coverlet of the hospital bed. She looks around at him. "Shall we give it another try, Gerald?"

3. *Country Girl.* This is the outdoor plot. Our girl on the farm has been courted for some time by True Blue Harold. Faithful as hell, but dull, dull, dull. She yearns to be swept off her feet. She is, by sophisticated, excruciatingly hand-

some Roderick, visitor from the city. Never was there such an emotional awakening down in the long grass by the millrace. But comes the cloudburst and the river is in spate. Either she, or the farm's valuable brood mare, is marooned out there beyond the surging torrent that the river has become. It doesn't really matter which. Somebody's got to be saved. It's the big scene, starting on page sixteen. And who does the saving? Roderick the City Slicker? Not on your life. It's good old Harold who swims out there and brings her or it back to safety, while Roderick just stands there looking sheepish. If ever a girl comes to the realization of True Worth in a man, this is it.

The other basic plots I have, mercifully, forgotten. But I do remember that I got to thinking that for the women who write this pap it was sure money. Why, I asked myself, shouldn't I churn out some of it and augment my salary, which was very much in need of it at the time. After all, it would be the easiest thing in the world because I knew the plots inside out.

So, at home I sat myself down at my typewriter to write one. But I had not got far before I felt that I was doing a tongue-in-cheek job. And I realized you couldn't make it sound right unless you brought to it some measure of sincerity. The thing is that the women who write it believe in it. They believe that it is they who have for the first time thought up the plot about, say, the not too good-looking girl who shares an apartment with a real glamour gal. . . . The poor ugly duckling feeling doomed for the shelf sees her girl friend go off night after night to have gay times while she sits at home trying to beat herself at Scrabble. But the glamorous one has a row with the terribly handsome man who is keen on her and one evening to show him where he gets off she decides to be out when he calls to take her to dinner. The stay-at-home does her best to make amends for her friend's bad manners. "Why don't I fix you something? We could eat here. It would be no trouble at all." And of course as he congratulates her on the superbly cooked meal she has whipped up and they are finishing off the bottle of California wine he realizes that here is the warm-hearted, sympathetic, intelligent, understanding, sincere sort of girl he should marry, rather than the glossy, artificial, flighty type that one is likely to get involved with.

It is a story of hope for all the stay-at-home ugly ducklings across the land. And as such it must be written with Heart, just like all the other women's short stories, which on analysis are seen to be fiction with a message, like the one about (I've remembered another) the woman who has broken with her husband and grants him nothing but visiting privileges to their young son and horses around with all sorts of men until one day she realizes the folly of it all when she overhears Junior say to a chum: "Tomorrow I'm seeing my *real* Daddy."

Such fictional balm for the marriage-on-the-rocks woman, frustrated homely girl, childless wife, mother with a problem child, etc., I could not write with the required amount of Heart, so reluctantly I had to pass up what I had thought would be a glorious chance to get on to a good thing.

Such fiction is by and for women and I suppose one should not be too critical of it. After all it is harmless enough and certainly not calculated to corrupt the mind. But viewing it all quite objectively, as long as so many females devote so much time to it the feminists are going to have a hard job convincing us that women are not a thing apart and on another level from men.

Conclusion

At the end of the long haul of doing research into what makes women tick I am left with the view that there is one factor which, more than any other single consideration, makes them indelibly women and which is the great stumbling block for those who would change their status, whether it be under the banner of liberation, equality, call it what you will.

This was vividly brought home to me, along with the television-viewing millions around the world, when there was a special TV program which was devoted to Germaine Greer's tour of the U.S. to promote her book, *The Female Eunuch*, and which contained shots of that pathetic Women's Lib rally in Washington in the spring of 1971. The fascinating aspect of this, apart from the pitiful turnout and the embarrassing performances of the platform speakers and propaganda singers, was the fact that all the police who cordoned the area to offset trouble were black. No trouble did materialize, for this very reason that it was an all-black security force. It was a brilliant piece of thinking on the part of the authorities, since they knew that the Women Libbers align themselves with the fight against oppression by the colored peoples (Gloria Steinem: "The blacks are our allies against the white male oppressor.") But the militant feminists demonstrating there in Washington were furious at this clever move to keep them under control. It was a dirty trick. And none felt more strongly about it than Germaine Greer, who was seen to burst into a flood of tears at the perfidy that had been worked upon them. And then as she walked dejectedly from the scene she turned to a friend and, by way of explanation of the tears still streaming down her face, she said: "I guess I've got my period coming."

For me, that nutshelled the whole futility of Women's Liberation. No matter how great the effort to achieve "freedom from sexual classification," women keep being reminded (and reminding *us*, as Greer did) that they are female and radically different.

A fervid feminist, to prove that she can stand side by side with men, may hold in check or with a conscious effort change such feminine indicators as: tears, giggling, getting in a tizzy, preoccupation with outward appearance from hairdo to toenail polish, inability to be logical, practical, and objective. But she is going along fine, really convincing herself and everybody around her—at the sales meeting, the medical convention, the political conference—that here is someone who fits naturally into the masculine setup, and then whambo!—menstruation. Abruptly she is reminded: "You're a woman, dear. You've got to take time out to be feminine."

You see, those things like tears, giggling, etc., are feminine characteristics only in degree. Men are often known to cry, they are capable of giggling, many of them are emotional, a lot of men are impractical, and so on. They are characteristics common to both sexes, but are regarded primarily as female traits merely because women display them more often and in a more highly developed form. But no man ever menstruates. This condition, with all its ramifications and its influences on those who undergo it, is a biological difference. And nobody can do anything about changing it.

So, what is the solution? The solution is what it has always been with the vast majority of women, despite the endeavors of emancipators, suffragettes, liberators, and other hotheads. Just get on with being a woman, find the contentment and the reflected happiness of being secondary to men. The really appealing women are those who set out to and make a good job of that.